MANAGING
SUBSURFACE
DATA IN THE OIL
AND GAS SECTOR
SEISMIC

SEISMIC

AHMAD BIN MAIDINSAR

PARTRIDGE

To order additional copies of this book, contact
Toll Free 800 101 2657 (Singapore)
Toll Free 1 800 81 7340 (Malaysia)
orders.singapore@partridgepublishing.com

www.partridgepublishing.com/singapore

CONTENTS

FIGURES

TABLES

FOREWORD

This guide book is a day to day monitor of handling seismic data. It is orientate to computer specialist who have constant interaction with the geoscientists in generating seismic projects in any system platforms in many different working environments

The book starts with the historical background on subsurface data management and definition of commonly occurring geotechnical terms and ends with data backups and archives which help saved the data for future reference. Data can come in different forms, media, and formats and the IT professionals (data managers) have to make these data available and usable for the end user (seismic interpreter, geologist, decision makers), depending on the company's purpose or requirements.

Nowadays with 64-bit machines which rendered faster speed and with cheap storage devices for huge data load, the data managers still have to understand the flow of the subsurface data management so as to make the data deem usable to the end-users.

To summarize, this guidebook is loaded with a wealth of useful tips for subsurface data management for data management personnels who support essentially the oil and gas business.

Dr. Vladimir Machado
PhD in Geosciences
Director—Exploration, SONANGOL P&P

APPRECIATION

I would like to take this opportunity to thank my family {mother, wife & kids for being patience during the whole period of revising this book.

And also not forgetting my friends from 14 countries in 29 sites globally that I've the pleasure to work with viz. Algeria (Algiers, Boumedes, Hassi Messaoud), Angola (Luanda), Brunei (Seria), Gabon (Gamba), Indonesia (Djakarta), Japan (Tokyo), Korea (Seoul), Malaysia (KL, Miri), Nigeria (Lagos, Port Harcourt, Warri), Singapore, Taiwan (Taipeh), The Netherlands (Rijswijk), Thailand (Bangkok), UK (England – Reading, Scotland – Aberdeen)

PREFACE

A simple guide for data managers who are in need of more control on the seismic data management and also provided a brief introduction to seismic in general for students of the Earth sciences faculties.

Within chapters, there are easy workflow to follow so as to have a good grip on the topics under discussions

With the increasing in volumes of the seismic data, data managers have to improvise ways and methods to 'protect' the data from getting adulterated with junk data.

Note that all seismic data on display are from public domains and some do have footnotes so as to provide information on the sources taken.

I – OVERVIEW

> *Make things happened …*
>
> *Don't wait for things to happen*

What is data?

That which provides info:

(1) to be processed
(2) to be utilized
(3) to be managed

> *Seismic Data Management –*
>
> *"A logical and systematic way to manage seismic data from the onset of receiving the data to archiving"*
>
> *No data, no project ©amsar58*

So a data manager manages everything pertaining to data, whether the data are petroleum-related or finance-related or human resource-related i.e. from A to Z.

It is a tough job but in life nothing is impossible.

But for this 'little' book, it is only the seismic-related data that we are interested in.

But what then is seismic?

Seismic are energy waves that pass through the Earth due to natural or unnatural sources or disturbances (e.g., earthquakes or explosions).

And what then is seismic data?

Seismic data are datasets resulting from these seismic waves in the form of wriggly lines (spaghetti-like) detected by receivers known as geophones (on land) or hydrophones (in a marine environment), depicting information about the Earth's subsurface. See **Figure I-1** for an example of seismic data.

Now, these are processed seismic data generated in SEGY format. SEGY is an abbreviation of Society of Exploration Geophysics format Y. The SEGY format will be explained in detail in **VI. SEGY Header Analysis**.

The raw, unprocessed, or field data are in SEGD format, and we are not going to touch this dataset because they are in the custody of the processing centers to be processed, and their output is in SEGY format.

Normally, the clients are given copies of the SEGD datasets for safekeeping, in the beginning, on 7 or 9-track tape, now normally on Linear – Tape – Open (LTO) media. As we speak, processing companies are probably finding ways to store these field data which in total size can be from the 50s to 100s depending on the extent of the "projects."

Throughout this book, we will only be dealing with seismic data in SEGY format.

Please note that now even other seismic attributes and well attributes are stored in SEGY format.

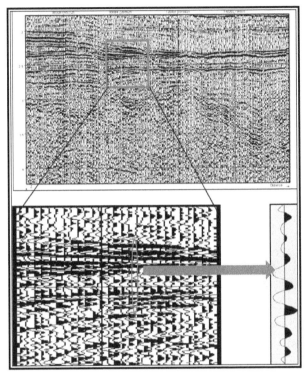

Figure I-1: Seismic section and a trace after undergoing processing[1]

In simple term, seismic data is an acoustically graphical representation of the geology of the Earth's subsurface.

And there is a pattern of how these waves are encapsulated i.e., through a series of predesign lines or traverse paths.

For a bit more on seismic and its acquisition, see **III. Seismic Surveys.**

---

[1] F3 3D seismic from OPENDTECT: www.opendtect.com

Now, these wriggly traces (as we call them and also known as signatures) are sinusoidal, i.e., having a series of curvatures (known as lobes) in which to the right is black-filled and to the left is white-filled as we have seen in the **Figure I-1**. This mode of display is what we call variable area + wiggle or, in short, just variable area, and the medium of display is usually paper or paper print.

It is only after processing that these curvatures have geological and geophysical meaning to them.

In geological terms, these black/white lobes are representations of each layering of the earth subsurface, be it limestone, shale, sand, gas, water.

Please do refer to a number of good books from basic to advance geology available in the market.

And in geophysical terms, the black lobes denote either a "hard-kick" or a "soft-kick" of a layer.

A "hard-kick" shows that the layer in focus has a "slower" or "softer" layer above it. A "soft-kick" shows that the layer in focus has a "faster" or "harder" layer above it.

For a bit more information on that wriggly-like trace, please refer to **VI. SEGY Header Analysis – Section Polarity**.

Before the advent of workstations for geophysics and geology (G & G), seismic data management is all about having to store seismic data on reel tapes from seismic acquisition (the way seismic data are captured) to seismic processing (the way seismic data are processed for final output to users).

For displays, we print seismic traces on papers for interpretation normally from films or even sepias.

The tapes were sent for safekeeping in the companies' "cold" storage facilities and the interpreted sections folded as part of the reports or placed in the box files for future reference.

In the late 1970s and early 1980s when G & G workstations were developed and undergoing further development and improvement, paper sections were still being used but to a lesser extent.

Paper seismic sections were scanned, and its digital – form loaded in the workstation has questionable accuracy in the record length i.e the vertical scale and the shotpoint-trace (SP – TR) intervals i.e. the horizontal scale due to stretching.

Currently with the latest in storage technology, terabyte, zettabytes, yottabytes[2] of data are being accessed, used, and archived in a matter of minutes.

This is where the basic understanding of seismic data management is needed to ensure that nothing is lost in the geophysical sense, right from seismic acquisition, seismic processing, data gathering, seismic interpretation, data back up, and right up to data archiving.

As the seismic acquisition, seismic processing, and seismic interpretation undergo advancement with new technology, the same goes with seismic data management.

We have to adapt in our approach to these advancements but the concept still remains.

To recollect, two standard formats seismic can be stored:

(1) SEGD: field data or unprocessed dataset
(2) SEGY: processed seismic dataset, again, as shown in **Figure I-1**.

---

[2] Maximum storage capacity defined by Julian Bunn et al., in his GIOD project.

Earlier on, say in the 1960s and 1970s, we have SEGA, SEGB, SEG-EX, and SEGC formats. More on SEGY later in **VI. SEG Header Analysis**.

> *Current technology ...*
>
> *Data can be accessed easily and rapidly but can be lost likewise*
> ©amsar58

So be wary in the data cleaning process as data might get deleted within minutes or even seconds.

We are going to discuss more on this data cleaning in **VIII. Data Harmonization**.

FLOW IN DATA MANAGEMENT

The flow below depicts the eight golden rules in data management.

The rules are nothing but to guide one in managing data professionally and efficiently.

1	DATA SEARCH, COLLECTION, GATHERING
2	DATA IDENTIFICATION, VERIFICATION, VALIDATION (CATALOGING, INDEXING, SCANNING, DIGITIZING)
3	DATA REPOSITORY, INPUT, LOAD
4	DATA VALIDATION, VERIFICATION OF THE INPUT
5	CLIENTS/END–USERS PARTICIPATION
6	CLIENTS/END–USERS APPROVAL
7	DATA BACKUPS–RESTORES
8	DATA ARCHIVE, STORAGE

Table I-1: Eight golden rules of data management flow

This flow forms the basis for this book with which we are going to elaborate in detail in **V. The FLOW: Data Management.**

We could have added #9, i.e., Data Security but this falls under the category of Information Technology (IT) Systems Infrastructure.

Firstly, we will touch base with a short history of the seismic data survey, storage media, and workstation which are in the following chapter.

There are many books in the market which are "tremendously" good in seismic acquisition, processing, and interpretation to be used as references, and some of them are given in the section – **Further reading** at the end of this chapter.

There are no big jargons used in this book, so anyone with tertiary education and some flair in IT can manage seismic data with minimal knowledge of geophysics or geology. For the Earth Sciences students, the book is one step further into a carer in the oil & gas industry.

But most importantly, recorded whatever jobs or tasks accomplished for the purpose of report writing for future references and also for audit trail.

Now let us get started.

FURTHER READING

	Title	Author	Date	Website
1	The GIOD Project (globally interconnected object database)	Julian J. Bunn[3][4] Koen Holtman[5] Harvey B. Newman[3] Richard P. Wilkinson[3]	2000	http://odbms.org/download/ Bunn The GIOD Project-Globally Interconnected Object Databases 2000.pdf
2	Recommended standards for digital tape formats: SEGA, SEGB, SEG-EX	Northwood, E. J., Weisinger, R. C., and Bradley,	1967	http://www.seg.org/resources/ publications/ misc/technical-standards
3	Recommended standards for digital tape formats: SEGC	Meiners, E. P., Lenz, L. L., Dalby, A. E. and Hornsby, J. M.	1972	http://www.seg.org/resources/ publications/ misc/technical-standards

---

[3] California Institute of Technology, Pasadena, USA
[4][5] CERN, Geneva, Switzerland

II – SEISMIC

Firstly, we go through a brief description of:

(1) Seismic Waves
(2) Seismic Storage Media
(3) Seismic Workstation

SEISMIC WAVES

Revision: Seismic waves are waves propagating through the earth due to natural causes (e.g., earthquakes) or unnatural causes (e.g., explosions).

Figure I-1 displays different modes of seismic waves that are detected during any acquisition;

(1) the reflection method now used in most of the seismic surveys for deeper detection of geologic features or hydrocarbon-bearing structures.
(2) the refraction method use to detect shallow features.
(3) the surface wave method performed prior to reflection seismic and also used for shallow regions.

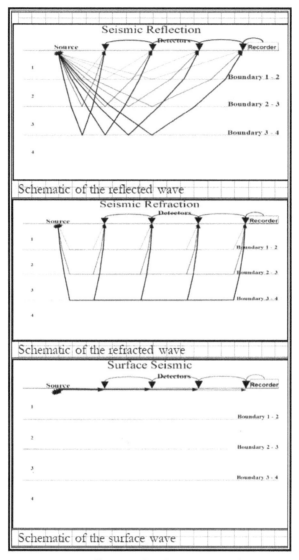

Figure II-1: Different modes of seismic waves detection

We are not going to go through in detail for the above methods in seismic surveys as there are numerous highly complimented, comprehensive, and recommended literatures on this subject.

Most of the SEGY data received in the Oil & Gas (O&G) industry are in the seismic reflection mode.

Table 2-1 briefly describes the mode of propagation for each type of wave.

Wave type	*Propagation mode*
P-wave	Travels along the wave train
S-wave	Travels perpendicular to the wave train
Love-wave	Travels along the wave train on the surface
Rayleigh-wave	Travels perpendicular to the wave train on the surface

Table II-1: Type of seismic waves

A SHORT INTRODUCTION TO SEISMIC WAVES

Remember the wiggly-trace in **Figure I-1**.

The three basic 'ingredients' in any sinusoidal waves (light, sound, seismic, … waves):

(1) Amplitude
(2) Frequency
(3) Wavelength

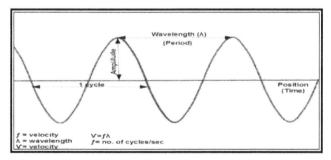

Figure II-2: A sinusoidal wave denoting (1) amplitude (2) frequency (3) wavelength

This sinusoidal wave tells stories:

(1) The amplitude shows the strength or intensity of the medium the wave is traveling in.
(2) While the wavelength indicates the type of medium the wave is traveling in.
(3) And the frequency tells us how many wave cycles for a given period passing through a medium which inadvertently reflects the kind of geology we are facing.

Waves travelling through various layers of the Earth will display ranges of amplitudes, frequencies, and wavelengths. Also, by getting the product of frequency and wavelength, we will obtain the velocity.

⇨   Frequency * wavelength
⇨ $f * \lambda$, since $f = 1/T$ and Wavelength = distance, D
⇨ $1/T * \lambda$
⇨ λ/T
⇨   distance/time
⇨   velocity, v

So $v = \lambda/T = f*\lambda$

For example, a wave traveling through solid will obviously display many peaks and troughs (i.e., more frequencies) as compared to a wave traveling through liquid within the same distance. And the measurement of frequency i.e. cycle per second, (Hz)

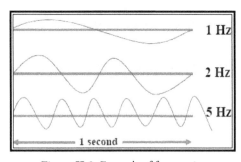

Figure II-3: Example of frequencies

SEISMIC STORAGE MEDIA

PAPER

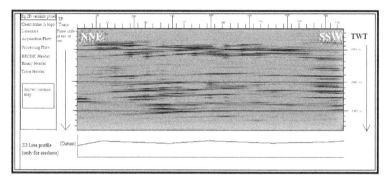

Figure II-4: Paper seismic section

Figure II-4 shows the final seismic section plotted on paper, generated by the processing center for the client.

The display mode generated for the final display is normally in the VAR, i.e., variable area for the seismic interpreters to work upon.

The line orientation is NNE (north north-east) to SSW (south south-west).

We can see from the left axis the value of two-way time until 3800ms.

In the later years for newer paper seismic print, you will see a table of Time Vs Vel (NMO) at every 50 or 100 cdp at the top of the seismic section above the SP – CD annotations.

It would be ideal if we could have such a display in our G&G workstation with the option to turn the Time - Velocity table ON or OFF at our disgression. Not only that, these tables should also be active so as to be able to generate RMS velocity and/or INTERVAL velocity for seismic Depth conversion.

FILM

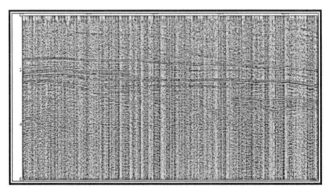

Figure II-5: Seismic section on film—an example

Figure II-5 shows seismic section on film in the early days of seismic interpretation on papers. These films are kept in long cylindrical canisters.

This type of medium is normally for

(1) storing the seismic section in order to reprint the seismic data and
(2) archiving the seismic section in the data library for future reference.

In color, the film should be very transparent thus it is necessary to keep them very well in order to preserve the print.

SEPIA

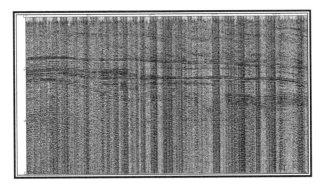

Figure II-6: Seismic section on sepia—an example

Figure II-6 shows another form of medium in the early days, i.e., 1960s, 1970s, and early 1980s.

These seismic sections were

(1) stored for further reprint and
(2) archived for future use or reference.

Nowadays, there are numerous contractors that provide services to scan the paper seismic to be converted into digital SEGY format. In color, the sepia can range from brownish – orange to yellowish – brown.

MICROFICHE (FLAT SHEETS)

A card or sheet of microfilm capable of accommodating and preserving a considerable number of pages, as of printed text, in reduced form.

Figure II-7: Microfiche

Figure II-7 shows an example of a microfiche. To read the microfiche, a microfiche reader is used.

Data are read by scrolling up and down left and right to display any sections of the microfiche.

MICROFILM (REELS)

Another set of medium for seismic storage and eventually will generate seismic paper sections for interpretations. The medium is in roll – form compared to the microfiche which is flat. Mind that this was the norm in the 1970s and still was in the early 1980s.

FLOPPY DISKS

Figure II-8: Floppy disk—8", 5¼", and 3½"

Normally, these floppies are used to store navigation data and WELL data in ASCII format, e.g., synthetic seismogram, time-depth table, well test, perforation, edited log curves, etc., of smaller bytes capacity. Since nowadays new generation laptops have no floppy reader, data on floppies are thus normally read on old laptops or old desktops.

It is a worthwhile project to copy the data from these floppies, as all data will be intact in the latest media they were copied onto. Preferably, use an optical-type disk as it will be very handy in terms of mobility and storage.

Note:

Make it a point to create a "special" project to convert all the data currently residing on floppies or other forms of old media, onto the more robust media, e.g., the up-to-date optical-type disk or hard drive.

The reasons being that many of the obsolete media-types are not readable by staffs and also by contractors due to lack of older tape drives and optical readers.

A bit of practical advice here:

(1) Keep a list of all data and their media of storage plus the date of creation.
(2) With the details of the equipment used, it will be useful when these data are to be read in the near future.
(3) Review the date (to check for readability, re-mastering and the usage for these data on these media). This should not exceed four to five [4–5] years as the media and their storage technology market moves incredibly fast.

Since nowadays new generation laptops have no floppy reader, data on floppies are thus normally read on old laptops or old desktops.

It is a worthwhile project to copy the data from these floppies, as all data will be intact in the latest media they were copied onto.

Preferably, use an optical-type disk as it will be very handy in terms of mobility and storage. The reasons being that many of the obsolete media-types are not readable by staffs and also by contractors due to lack of older readers.

Nowadays, there are hardly any laptops or notebooks that have the floppy device installed. But we do have external device for reading floppies if they are still compatible with the latest Windows/Macs OS, i.e., operating systems.

TAPES

i. Reel Tapes

Figure II-9: ½" Tape (9 – track)

Family:
— Half – inch 9 – track
— 7 – track
— 21 – track

The 7 and 9 – track tape is widely used in the 80s and early 90s for storing seismic data 2D data and the navigation data. Initially, one seismic line was recorded on the tape until in the 90s whereby multiple seismic lines were embedded in the tape.

These tapes were maintained by using tape cleaning alcohol at regular interval.

The initial 21-track & 7-track tape (200, 556 and 800 BPI) were replaced by the 9-track tape (open reel 800, 1600, 3200, and 6250 BPI).

ii. Cartridge Tapes

a. ¼" cartridge

Figure II-10: Cartridge types

Among the earliest medium used to backup SEGY output to be sent to partners, for incremental backups and to store OS (operating system) to be used for installation for some computer vendors.

b. Exabyte

Figure II-11: Digital Linear Tape

Family;

— 4 mm DDS (Digital Data Storage), 4 mm HP DAT, 8mm DL (Digital Linear), 8mm AME (Advance Metal Evaporated Mammoth), DLT (Digital Linear Tape), SDLT (Super Digital Linear Tape), LTO (Linear Tape Open)

Tape medium used to transport the SEGY-formatted seismic data and also for project backups and archival in the 90s and still currently used especially the DLTs and the LTOs.

OPTICAL DISKS

Figure II-12: Types of Optical disks

Family:

— CDR, DVD – RW, Magneto optical, Dual Layer Blu-ray

The medium is used to work online and taken off from the system at the end of the day for safe-keeping. Used for SEGY input – output and for final total backup for projects.

The Magneto is used to work online and taken off from the system at the end of the day for safe-keeping.

MASS STORAGE

The medium is used for incremental backups and restores on a daily basis, e.g. if files on the computer systems are accidently deleted or get corrupted.

The cartridge or capsule as we would like to call is read by a robotic-type sorter which is used to access the cartridge during one of its routine tasks.

http://en.wikipedia.org/wiki/Mass_Storage_System.

WESTERN DIGITAL (WD) HARD DRIVE

Figure II-13: WD 8Tb hard-drive

Figure II-18 are 2Tb hard drives from WD used for transporting SEGY seismic data from processing Companies to clients. Currently, one of the popularly used media in data storage and transfer. This has now becoming a trend whereby data from 'old' media are being transcribe onto the 1 or 2Tb hard disks, now even upto 8Tb.

News have it that IBM has started building (in 2011) the world's largest data repository setup totaling up to 120 petabyte which is equivalent to 120 million gigabytes.

LATEST TECHNOLOGY

Researches on data storage have been done and still ongoing on these three methods below (to name a few):

(1) DNA storage method [5]
(2) Molecular storage method[6]
(3) Photo-polymerization method[7]

Even though we have yet to see the final patent and also these methods are in the process of collating views, the future for these techniques are not too far.

Upon success, we can see the:

(1) ability to store a billion copies of a ~50,000-word book fitting into the equivalent of moisture at the bottom of a small tube or glass
(2) ability to store data at a density of 1,000 terabytes per square inch with a nanometer in size
(3) ability to store 1 petabyte data on a DVD-size polymer disk

With all these new storage technologies, the question is "can the seismic data be stored without compromising the speed of retrieval and backup," as we all know that one seismic file can be as large as 500GB or now 1TB?

---

[5] George Church & European Bioinformatics Institute (EBI)
[6] Massachusetts Institute of Technology (MIT)
[7] Swinburne University of Technology and CSIRO (the Commonwealth Scientific and Industrial Research Organization, Australia

WORKSTATION

Figure II-14: Workstation_seismic interpretation

Figure II-15: Workstation_geological interpretation

Figure II-14 shows an example of a standard up-to-date workstation—dual screen for the oil and gas sector. Here seismic workstation can be for seismic interpretation and **Figure II-15** for geological interpretation.

The normal workstation set up is dual screen and can go up to four screens depending on how many graphic card slots one has. The hardware will vary in terms of CPU speed and RAM capacity. Also not to forget, the size of the screen.

For the Operating system (OS), we can either have dual booting, i.e., Windows and Linux or either one installed, with the other virtual. But bear in mind that running some software on either platform might encounter some problems especially those which has something to do with graphics.

Now the work can be performed on high RAM laptops.

FURTHER READINGS

	Title	Author	Date	Website
1	A brief history of tape.	Lynne Avery	Mar 2000	www.exabyte.com www. mammothtape.com
2	Computer Peripherals	Third year undergraduate course–Nanyang Technological University, Singapore		www.lintech.org
3	History of Seismology	Naar – jorden – skleker	19 Feb 2010	www.geo.uib. no.nnsn.nnar-jorden-skjelver/contents/ en/history.html
4	A New Approach To Information Technology, Communications of the ACM, Vol. 56 No. 8, Pages 13-15	Samuel Greengard	Aug 2013	http://cacm.acm.org/ magazines/ 2013/8/166306-a-new-approach-to-information-storage/ fulltext
5	New technique would allow a petabyte of data on a single disk	Brian Dodson	8 Jul 2013	http://www.gizmag. com/petabyte-dvd-data-storage/28181/

III – SEISMIC SURVEYS

Before we go into the seismic surveys proper, let us briefly touch on the sequence of events that will finally lead us onto getting our seismic data.

As an example, say we have a company named Global Exploration Pte. Ltd[8]. The company is always looking, searching, and exploring for oil and gas worldwide, not to mention refining and producing O&G products.

We just got the license for an area to explore and produce (what is known as "farm-in").

The terms and conditions warrant us to explore and produce for 20 years, i.e., 5 years exploration and 15 years for production if our company successfully detects a humongous reserve or pockets of reserves straddling across the area, an example.

The farm-in area might be a virgin area or an area where some explorations have been performed earlier as shown as an example in **Figure III-1**. Note that the well name and the lease plate information have been added just as an example.

---

[8] An example of O&G Company

Figure III-1: Farm-in area—BLOCK 12/15

For a virgin area, no seismic surveys whatsoever have been performed plus no wells have been drilled.

So we have to start from scratch, i.e., go back to the drawing board to plan and design or 'sketch' our new seismic survey – pre-survey design(normally and initially 2D seismic surveys).

At times we do find contractors that have performed extensive surveys over the areas for data-sales to intended farm-in O&G companies interested. Normally they will sell these block per block depending on the agreement they had concluded with the Authorities of the country.

Also, we could have other non-seismic data like aero-magnetic or gravity survey for the area.

SURVEY TYPE

Figure III-2 and **Figure III-3** display schematically how seismic data are acquired.

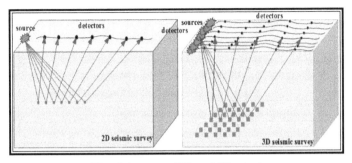

Figure III-2: Schematic of 2D and 3D seismic survey

In **Figure 3-2**, notice the 2D survey has only a single linear data collection point, whereas the 3D has multiple linear data collection points.

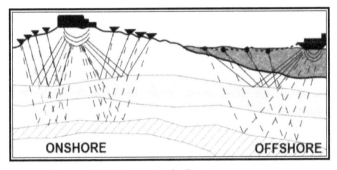

Figure III-3: Schematic of reflection seismic survey
onshore (LHS) and offshore (RHS)

The principles behind the seismic acquisition for both onshore and offshore are similar and applicable for both 2D and 3D surveys.

The differences are only in the

(1) Logistics
(2) placement of the receivers (onshore).
(3) the boat traverse settings (offshore).
(4) seismic datum.

Some of the seismic sources for the seismic surveys are of the following:

	Sources	Website
1	Explosives	http://www.aryum.com/ products-and-applications/explosives
2	Thumper	http://www.utexas.edu/
3	Airgun	http://www.norwalkcitizenonline.com//
4	Watergun	http://www.geoexpro.com/

These are the sources used in onshore or transitional zones surveys.

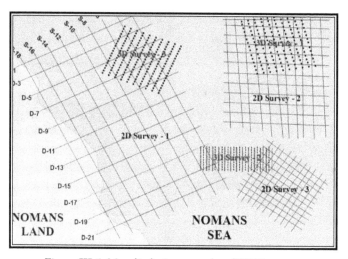

Figure III-5: Map displaying examples of 2D3D surveys

Figure III-5 displays three [3] 3D surveys and a series of lines representing three [3] 2D surveys.

Looking at the 2D lines, we could see that the surveys are of different grids. The 2D survey on the LHS of the picture has obviously bigger grids than the surveys to the RHS. The 2D lines overlapping with the 3D survey (to the south) have tighter grids compared to the other 2D surveys in the picture.

In areas deprived of 3D, one could see 2D surveys prevailed from early acquisitions. 2D surveys are now being used less and less except for regional interpretation or to delineate areas where there are no 3D surveys.

Due to the confidentiality of the data, there is no easting/northing or LAT/LON on the map.

2D SURVEY

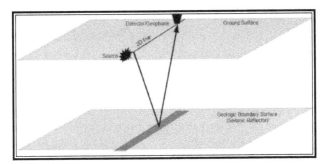

Figure III-6: 2D seismic survey operation

Figure III-6 depicts a schematic diagram of how 2D line in a survey was acquired. The subsurface information (or geology in the real sense) will be reflected on each line traversed only.

See **Figures III-6** and **III-8**.

Here two (2) entities are registered:

(1) Seismic data.
(2) Navigation data, i.e., location of the detectors receiving the seismic signals.

More of these in **III. Seismic Surveys** on page 43 and **IV. Coordinate Reference Systems**.

These data acquired will be sent to the seismic processing center for further "refinement" so that the final output will be used by the users (i.e., seismic interpreters).

Figure III-7: Central Alaska—2D seismic lines visualized in 3D viewer[9]

Figure III-7 shows a 3D image view of 2D seismic lines.

Subsurface data are represented below the acquired lines. In between the lines, there is no subsurface image. Since data are acquired below each shot-point (SP), thus a single 2D line comprises of a series of SP. See **Figure III-8**.

If we were to plot every SP in the surveys, (1) on the plotter, the ink might run out, and (2) on the workstation, we will have slowness in displaying our base-map and also our seismic lines.

That is why we always see maps plotted every 500 to 1000 SP for small-scale maps (1:100000 or 1:250000) and every 100 to 200 SP even at times 40/50 SP for big scale maps (1:10000 or 25000).

Figure III-8 depicts a portion of the 2D lines in circle of how the shot-points are represented if the scaling of the map is enlarged.

---

[9] Software used – OPENDTECT (www.opendtect.com)

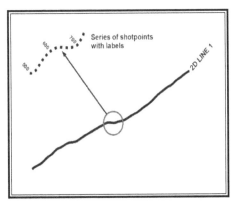

Figure III-8: Shot-point (SP) representation of a 2D line on a
base-map with each SP registering X and Y coordinates

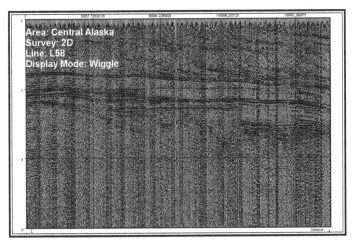

Figure III-9: Central Alaska—2D survey – line
58 in variable area + wiggle display mode

Figure III-9 shows line 58 of the 2D survey in a display mode what we
call wiggle trace or variable area trace.

It's just a presentation in black and white. This is the seismic section
we'll get before the advent of the G&G workstation.

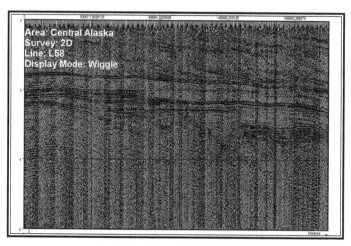

Figure III-10: Central Alaska 2D survey—line 58
in variable density + wiggle display mode

With the advent of the G&G workstation, lines can be displayed in various modes and colors. See **Figure III-10**. These assist the interpreters to further analyze their seismic datasets.

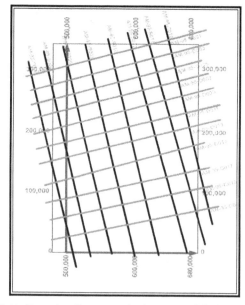

Figure III-11: Example of base-map displaying simplified 2D survey lines

Figure III-11 is a simplified version of a 2D survey with simple line nomenclature, e.g., AM – 95 – D019, AM – 95 – 010.

For 2D surveys, there are lines known as dip-lines and strike-lines plus few regional lines that connect one survey area to the other. This will assists in delineating structure from one area to another.

The dip-lines (black in color) are lines that straddle across structures or fault planes. This is only an example as the orientation can vary.

The strike-lines (grey in color) are lines that run parallel to the structures or fault planes.

The 2D surveys are contained by the XY coordinate values of the shot points (SP). More details in **IV. Coordinate Reference Systems**.

Newly farm-in companies will use these 2D surveys to re-examined "old" interpretation so as to have preliminary understanding of the structures prior to proposing their exploration and development programs.

Prior to the advent of 3D visualization, interpreters have to deal with multiple screens, i.e., one window displaying the seismic data and another window displaying the base-map.

New technology now makes it possible to have multiple windows or tabs or scenes on one screen.

2D SURVEYS LINE NOMENCLATURE

2D Linename naming		
06 – 80 – 23		LINENAME
1	6	Block number
	80	Year of survey (acquisition)
	23	Line number
CR91 – 10		LINENAME
2	CR	Area name
	91	Year of survey (acquisition)
	10	Line number
01 – 88 – 201R		LINENAME
3	1	Block number
	88	Year of survey (acquisition)
	201	Line number
	R	Reshoot line
AA – 00 – 10A		LINENAME
4	AA	Area name
	0	Year of survey (acquisition)
	10	Line number
	A, B, C, D, ...	Line extension

Table III-1: Examples of some standard naming convention

Reshoot lines are normally due to weathering on the high seas, i.e., there's bad weather, and the waves swell.

Line extensions are normally due to system failure at the near end of the traverse line or to cover extra line folds or distances.

Bear in mind that we cannot get a 100% straight line in 2D surveys either onshore or offshore.

The obvious answer why that is:

(1) for offshore, it's either the weather which will affect the sea current or obstacle such as fish traps, and
(2) for onshore, the concerns will be the undulating surface and communal areas.

3D SURVEY

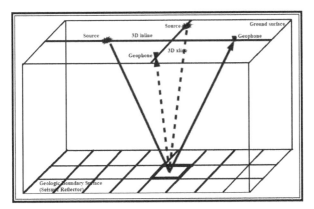

Figure III-12: 3D Seismic survey—operation

Due to the way the 3D data are acquired, subsurface information (i.e., the geology) will be depicted in all three axes. See **Figure III-12**. The concept behind 3D survey is that the seismic data provide information for the subsurface data in three-dimension, i.e., X-plane, Y-plane, and Z-plane.

The XY-planes which are vertical planes are represented by the INLINE and the XLINE. The Z-plane which is the horizontal plane is represented by the TIMESLICE. See **Figure III.13**. The 3D project survey is then defined by the four (4) corner points of the survey even if the live seismic traces covered are in irregular polygonal shape. See **Figure III.17**.

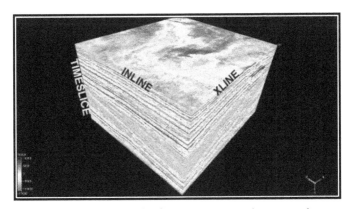

Figure III-13: Example of 3D seismic in visualization mode

Figure III-13 shows a typical 3D seismic data in volume mode.

Due to the acquisition settings, the seismic data are represented in a 3D cube.

The pricing of such acquisition warrants that:

(1) the 3D survey is implemented in areas where the potentials of discovering hydrocarbons are high especially if we have Direct Hydrocarbon Indicator (DHI); and
(2) to delineate also features that cannot be displayed in the 2D surveys.

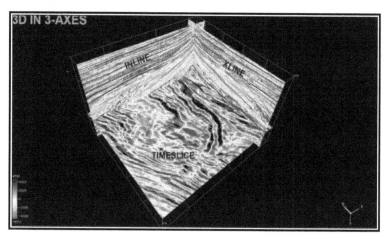

Figure III-14: Example of 3D seismic in planar
mode—INLINE, XLINE, and Z

Figure III-14 shows 3D seismic data in 3 planes coexist, i.e., inline plane, cross-line plane, and the time-plane which is better known as the time-slice.

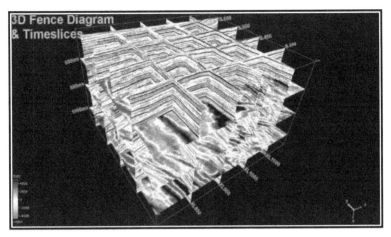

Figure III-15: 3D surveys in 3D view multiple IL, XL, and Z

Figure III-15 displays a fence diagram of the 3D seismic data as one of the visualization modes.

Figure III-16 shows an example of all the traces displayed in the 3D survey plus the zoom-in portion of the 3D survey.

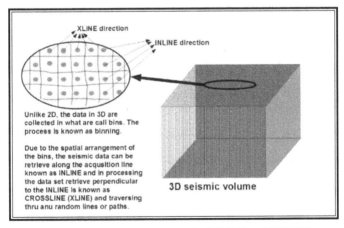

Figure III-16: Bins representing the INLINE and XLINE[10]

[10] Courtesy of Global Data Sub-Surface

If we were to display all the traces on all the ILINES, then we'd *only* see a square, rectangular, or polygonal shape in the base-map depicting these traces. So for viewing and working purposes, the basemap are displayed with increment in the INLINES and XLINES

Likewise in 2D surveys, 2 entities are registered in 3D surveys;

(1) Seismic data (in volumes – INLINES, XLINES & TIMESLICES
(2) Location at the point of data received, i.e., the detectors. But being a 3D volume, the location is captured within what we call "bins" which have XY stored in the system.

XY/INLINE/XLINE FOR THE SURVEY AREA DEFINITION

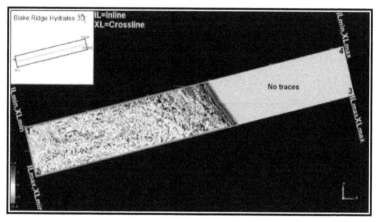

Figure III-17: 3D survey definition overlay map on TIMESLICE

IL (INLINE)	XL (XLINE)	X (EASTING)	Y (NORTHING)
1	1	430578.4	3527675.7
1	1306	478094.4	3539380.7
95	1	432265.4	3520830.7
95	1306	479781.4	3532535.7

Table III-2: Definition of four (4) corners of the 3D survey in terms of INLINE and XLINE

Table III-2 shows the definition of the survey based on the four (4) corner points.

Corner points	X	Y
1	430578.4	3527675.7
2	478094.4	3539380.7
3	432265.4	3520830.7
4	479781.4	3532535.7

Table III-3: 4 corner points of the 3D survey

INLINE/XLINE RANGE

IL: Min–max (above example; 1–95)
XL: Min–max (above example; 1–1306)

Although the active traces are in polygonal shape, the 3D surveys still have to be defined as a rectangular shape! See **Figure III-17**.

Theses parameters are normally set in the pre-survey phase or during the designing of the survey acquisition.

PROJECT/SURVEY DATUM

It is a reference datum whereby we measured times or depths from, in the seismic section. Time (T) = 0 ms and Depth (Z) = 0 m(ft).

But normally we make the reference datum = 0 measured from Mean-Sea-Level (MSL).

For offshore it is very clear-cut, seismic datum = 0 and the reference datum = 0 from MSL.

But for onshore, seismic datum = 300 (an example) or any other values, and the reference datum = 0 from MSL. This will either be in the Report either or both Acquisition and Processing or in the SEGY headers especially in the Trace header.

This is due to what the geophysicist term as the weathered layering above the reference datum.

This is an important piece of information where one should put in the seismic loading parameter for onshore data.

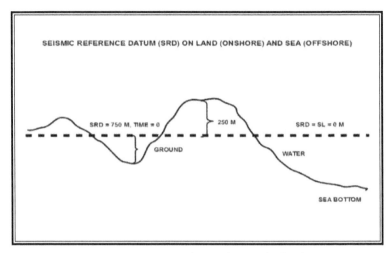

Figure III-18: Seismic reference datum – land and sea

Please do not get confused with the Coordinate Reference System datum which will be dealt in **IV. Coordinate Reference System**.

COMPOSITE LINES

In the "old days" (3D surveys), data managers used to received SEGY seismic with Inline values and Crossline values imbedded or merged together in one byte location for example;

Inline = 17500
Xline = 1350

And these values are represented as 175001350 (byte location 189, 4 – byte) in the Composite lines. And one way to segregate these values during loading is to define the byte locations as 2 – byte, not the normal

4 – byte that is for Inline used byte location 189, 2 – byte and for Xline used byte location 191, 2 – byte.

Line Type	Byte size	Byte location	Values
Composite	4 – byte	189	175001350
Separate into inline and xline			
Inline	2 – byte	189	17500
Xline	2 – byte	191	1350

FURTHER READINGS

	Title	Author	Date	Website
1	What is Seismic Survey	Park Seismic LLC		www.parkseismic.com/Whatisseismicsurvey.html
2	What is a seismic survey	Midwest Regional Carbon Sequestrian Partnership	Mar – 10	www.mrcsp.org
3	Seismic Surveys	Resolution Resources International		www.rri-seismic.com
4	Lease & Seismic	U.S. Emerald Energy Company, LP		www.usemeraldenergy.com

IV – COORDINATE REFERENCE SYSTEMS

How well the seismic is processed and how good is the interpretation, if the surveys are defined with the *wrong* coordinate reference system (CRS) it will result in the wrong location?

The wonderful work we have performed is meaningless or virtually comes to nothing.

Our goal here is how to define our survey correctly, whereby the seismic data will be loaded where the actual geology is and, in other words, where it should be.

SO WHAT IS COORDINATE REFERENCE SYSTEM (CRS)?

Before we get to know what CRS is, let's go through a simple exercise about navigation (or CRS) or in layman's term, where we are supposed to be, location-wise.

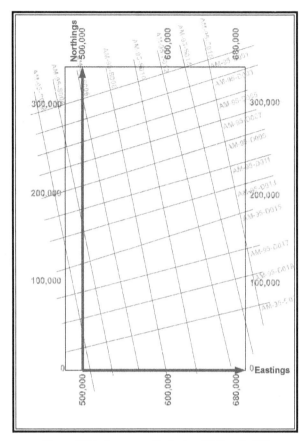

Figure IV-1: Base-map displaying 2D lines in XY
coordinates - ©Global Data Subsurface

Figure IV-1 shows a map in easting and northing. By looking at the
map, one can never be sure of where is the location of the 2D survey
lines.

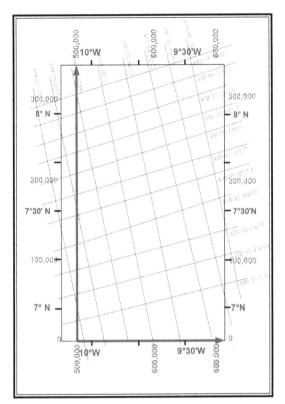

Figure IV-2: Basemap displaying 2D lines in XY coordinates with Latitude and Longitude overlay - ©Global Data Subsurface

But once the latitude (LAT) and longitude (LON) are denoted, then the location of the 2D survey lines can be readily identified as shown in **Figure IV-2**.

So **coordinate reference system** is a system to define a location on a map in XY coordinate system (meter/feet) transform from the LATLON (LL) system (DEG: MIN: SEC). The former is also known as projected coordinate reference system while the latter is known as geographic coordinate reference system.

LL is a representation of a global location whereby XY is a representation of a localized plane known as projected coordinates.

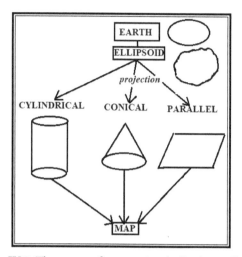

Figure IV-3: The process of representing the Earth on a flat map

Figure IV-3 depicts the flow of generating maps from the global reference system (or geographic coordinate system [LATLON]) to the localized system (or projected coordinate reference system [XY]).

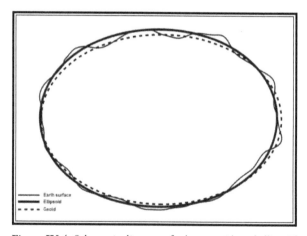

Figure IV-4: Schematic diagram of sphere, geoid, and ellipsoid

In layman's term;

Geoid: The surface that best fitted the surface of the Earth's mean sea level.

Ellipsoid (Spheroid): The surface that best fitted a localized area or plane of interest.

Datum: This determines which CRS systems used.

For example, concessions that have data extending across different CRS, care should be taken for the right CRS to be used.

See **VIII. Data Harmonization** on page **137** and decide on which CRS should be applied.

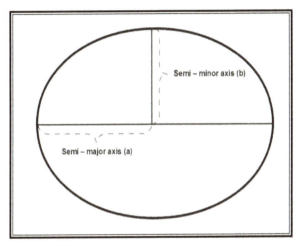

Figure IV-5: An ellipsoid – to represent the Earth surface

NAVIGATION—XY FOR THE LINE

Locations of the line(s) in the 2D surveys are determined by the coordinates system in terms of easting (X) and northing (Y), i.e., Cartesian coordinates.

Figures IV-6 – IV-12 show the 2d and 3D navigation formats which are in UKOOA (United Kingdom Offshore Operators Association) format.

P1/90

UKOOA P1/90 2D NAV FORMAT		
H0100	SURVEY AREA	
H0102	VESSEL DETAILS	
H0103	SOURCE DETAILS	
H0104	STREAMER DETAILS	
H0200	SURVEY DATE	
H0201	TAPE DATE (D.M.Y.)	
H0202	TAPE VERSION	
H0203	LINE PREFIX	
H0300	CLIENT	
H0400	GEOPHYSICAL CONTRACTOR	
H0500	POSITIONING CONTRACTOR	
H0600	POSITIONING PROCESSING	
H0700	POSITIONING SYSTEM	
H0800	SHOTPOINT POSITION	
H0900	OFFSET SHIP SYSTEM TO SP	
H1000	CLOCK TIME	
H1400	GEODETIC DATUM SURVEYED	
H1401	TRANSFORMATION PARAMETERS	
H1500	GEODETIC DATUM AS PLOTTED	
H1501	TRANSFORMATION PARAMETERS	
H1600	DATUM SHITS	
H1700	VERTICAL DATUM	
H1800	PROJECTION	
H1900	ZONE	
H2000	GRID UNITS	
H2001	HEIGHT UNITS	
H2002	ANGULAR UNITS	
H2100	STANDARD PARALLELS	
H2200	CENTRAL MERIDIEN	
H2301	GRID ORIGIN	
H2302	GRID COORDINATES AT ORIGIN	
H2600	BASE STATION 1	
H2600	BASE STATION ...	
H2600	BASE STATION ...	
H2600	BASE STATION ...	
H2600	ARGO LANE WIDTH	
H2600	DEPTH DATA REDUCTION	
H2600	...	
H2600	...	

Figure IV-7: Example—UKOOA P1/90 2D navigation format

Figure IV-7 shows an example of the dataset using the format for 2D surveys while **Figure IV-8** shows an example of the dataset using the format for 3D surveys.

UKOOA P1/90 3D NAV FORMAT	
H0100	SURVEY AREA
H0102	VESSEL DETAILS
H0102	VESSEL DETAILS
H0103	SOURCE DETAILS
H0103	SOURCE DETAILS
H0103	SOURCE DETAILS
H0103	SOURCE DETAILS
H0104	STREAMER DETAILS
H0104	STREAMER DETAILS
H0104	STREAMER DETAILS
H0104	STREAMER DETAILS
H0106	OTHER DETAILS
H0200	SURVEY DATE
H0201	TAPE DATE (D.M.Y.)
H0202	TAPE VERSION
H0300	CLIENT
H0400	GEOPHYSICAL CONTRACTOR
H0500	POSITIONING CONTRACTOR
H0600	POSITIONING PROCESSING
H0700	POSITIONING SYSTEM
H0800	SHOTPOINT POSITION
H0900	OFFSET SHIP SYSTEM TO SP
H0901	OFFSET ANTENNA TO SYSTEM
H0900	OFFSET SHIP SYSTEM TO SP
H0901	OFFSET ANTENNA TO SYSTEM
H1000	CLOCK TIME
H1100	RECEIVER GROUPS PER SHOT
H1400	GEODETIC DATUM SURVEYED
H1401	TRANSFORMATION PARAMETERS
H1500	GEODETIC DATUM AS PLOTTED
H1501	TRANSFORMATION PARAMETERS
H1600	DATUM SHITS
H1601	DATUM SHITS
H1700	VERTICAL DATUM
H1800	PROJECTION
H1900	ZONE
H2000	GRID UNITS
H2001	HEIGHT UNITS
H2002	ANGULAR UNITS
H2200	CENTRAL MERIDIEN
H2600	...
H2600	...
H2600	...
H2600	...
H2600	...

Figure IV-8: Example—UKOOA P1/90 3D navigation format

P6/98 (3D BIN)

	UK00A P6/98 3D BIN	
H0100	3D Survey Area	
H0200	Bin Grid Descriptor	
H0300	Geodetic Datum Name	
H0400	Ellipsoid-Axis-Inv Flat	
H0500	Projection Method	
H0510	Projection Zone Name	
H0530	Lon of CM (dms E/W)	
H0600	Descr of Linear Units	
H0700	Descr of Angular Units	
H0800	Bin Grid Origin (Io, Jo)	
H0900	Bin Grid Origin (E, N)	
H1000	Scale Factor at (I, J)	
H1100	Nom Bin Width on I axis	
H1150	Nom Bin Width on J axis	
H1200	Grid Bear J axis (dms)	
H1300	Bin Node Increment I axis	
H1350	Bin Node Increment J axis	
H1400	Coords (I, J, E, N) Fst Node	
H1401	Coords (Lat, Lon) Fst Node	
H1410	Coords (I, J, E, N) Sec Node	
H1420	Coords (I, J, E, N) Gen Pnt	
H2300	Data Extent Bin Grid	
H2400	Data Extent Map Grid	
H2501	Data Extent Bin Geog (N/S)	
H2502	Data Extent Bin Geog (E/W)	
H2700	Number of Prameters	
H2801	Total Coverage # of Nodes	
H2901	Total Coverage (I, j, E, N)	
H2901	Total Coverage (I, j, E, N)	
H2901	Total Coverage (I, j, E, N)	
H2901	Total Coverage (I, j, E, N)	
H2901	Total Coverage (I, j, E, N)	
H2901	Total Coverage (I, j, E, N)	
H2901	Total Coverage (I, j, E, N)	
H2901	Total Coverage (I, j, E, N)	
H2901	Total Coverage (I, j, E, N)	
H2901	Total Coverage (I, j, E, N)	
H2901	Total Coverage (I, j, E, N)	
H3102	Full Fold Cov # of Nodes	
H3202	Full Fold Cov (I, j, E, N)	
H3202	Full Fold Cov (I, j, E, N)	
H3202	Full Fold Cov (I, j, E, N)	
H3202	Full Fold Cov (I, j, E, N)	
H3202	Full Fold Cov (I, j, E, N)	
H3202	Full Fold Cov (I, j, E, N)	
H3202	Full Fold Cov (I, j, E, N)	
H3202	Full Fold Cov (I, j, E, N)	
H3202	Full Fold Cov (I, j, E, N)	
H3202	Full Fold Cov (I, j, E, N)	
H3202	Full Fold Cov (I, j, E, N)	
H3302	Full Fold Cov (I, j, E, N)	
H3403	Null Full Fold Cov # of Nodes	
H3503	Null Full Fold Cov (I, j, E, N)	
H3503	Null Full Fold Cov (I, j, E, N)	
H3503	Null Full Fold Cov (I, j, E, N)	
H3503	Null Full Fold Cov (I, j, E, N)	
H3503	Null Full Fold Cov (I, j, E, N)	
H3503	Null Full Fold Cov (I, j, E, N)	
H3503	Null Full Fold Cov (I, j, E, N)	
H3503	Null Full Fold Cov (I, j, E, N)	
H3503	Null Full Fold Cov (I, j, E, N)	

Figure IV-12: Example—UKOOA P6/98 3D Bin format

Take note that each navigation operator has its own internal format for raw navigation, e.g., WISDOM which is a proprietary navigation format for Western Geophysical in the 1990s.

WORLD UTM ZONATION NUMBER

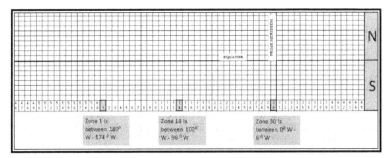

Figure IV-13: World UTM zone number

Figure IV-13 shows the UTM zonation globally. Each zone span across 6° (degrees) in longitude range and divided into 2 subzones, i.e., north (N) and south (S).

Thus, 30N or 30S is between 6° and 0°W and the central meridian is 3°E (+3°).

DEFINING LOCAL PROJECTION SYSTEM FOR A PROJECT

Prior to inputting data (see **VII. Seismic Data Loading** on page **129**), in all G&G software we will be requested to create a CRS for the seismic projects we are going to manage.

The basic key parameters are:

Parameters	Variables	Ellipsoid Dimensions	
		Semi Major Axis (a)	Inverse Flattening (1/f)
Projections Coordinate System	a) ED50 b) TRAVERSE MERCATOR c) UNIVERSAL TRAVERSE MERCATOR d) LAMBERT 2 PARALLEL		
Prime Meridiem	GREENWICH		
Datum	a) BEKOK b) CAMACUPA c) EUROPEAN DATUM 1950 d) KERTAU		
Ellipsoid	AUSTRALIAN 1965	6378160.0	298.250
	KRASOVSKY 1940	6378245.0	298.300
	CLARKE 1880	6378249.1	293.465
	CLARKE 1886	6378206.4	294.980
	INTERNATIONAL 1924 HAYFORD 1909	6378388.0	297.000
	AIRY 4 1830	6377563.4	299.320
	BESSEL 1841	6377397.2	299.150
	EVEREST 1830	6377276.3	300.800
	WGS 1972	6378135.0	298.260
	WGS 1984	6378137.0	298.257223563
Measurements	a. FEET b. METERS		
UTM Zones	Ranging from: a) 1N – 180N (=) b) 1S – 180S (=)		

Table IV-1: Parameters to define local CRS.

For more examples of these please see **Appendix D: Known Projection Systems** on pages **173**.

> *When defining the local datum, please ensure that the correct parameters have been keyed-in.*
>
> *This will determine the location of XY coordinates input are correct in values navigation-wise.*

EXERCISES ON CORRECT COORDINATES

EXERCISE IV.1: PLEASE DEFINE THE 3D SURVEY IN UTM Z10

Data are input correctly with the right XY values and in the correct coordinate reference system.

The correct coordinates are the resultant of the correct coordinate reference system applied.

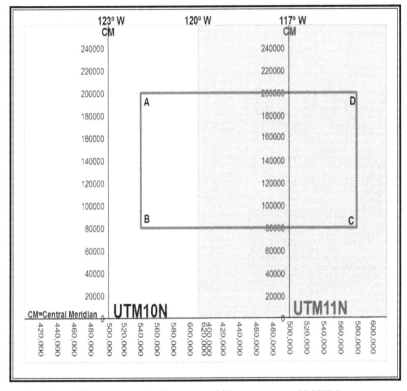

Figure IV-15: Example of survey straddling across two (2) UTM zones

(1) Standard 3D surveys with orientation EW
(2) 2 corner points of the 3D survey are in UTM10N zone while the other 2 are in UTM11N zone.

If the project defined in UTM10N, then for a 3D survey all the corner points is calculated with reference to UTM10N including points C and D.

Likewise, if a project defined in UTM11N, then this 3D survey's corners points are define in UTM11N.

UTM Zone	Corner	X	Y
10	A	540 000.00	200 000.00
10	B	540 000.00	80 000.00
10	C	800 000.00	80 000.00
10	D	800 000.00	200 000.00

Table IV-2: XY coordinates in UTM zone 10 for the survey corners

Don't get caught by inputting;

Corner C (X: <u>580 000.00</u> Y: 80 000.00) and
Corner D (X: <u>580 000.00</u> Y: 200 000.00)

EXERCISE IV.2: PLEASE DEFINE THE 3D SURVEY IN UTM Z11

UTM Zone	Corner	X	Y
11	A		
11	B		
11	C		
11	D		

Table IV-3: Exercise for the XY coordinates in zone 11 for the survey corners

> *Whatever the orientations of the 3D surveys, as long as we keep to the UTM zone, we are going to work i.e. the destination zone, we are saved!*

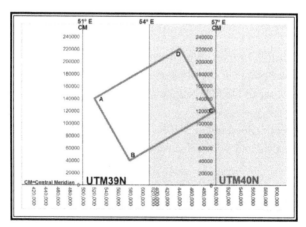

Figure IV-16: Example of survey straddling across two (2) UTM zones, i.e., Zone 39 and Zone 40

In the exercises, we only dealt with the UTM projection system as it is simple to follow.

With the advent of cartographic software, it is faster to perform cartographic conversion on other projection systems.

EXERCISE IV.3: PLEASE DETERMINE THE COORDINATES FOR THE CORNER POINTS A, B, C, AND D FOR BOTH ZONES IN FIGURE 4-16.

UTM Zone	Corner	X	Y
39	A		
39	B		
39	C		
39	D		
40	A		
40	B		
40	C		
40	D		

Table IV-4: Exercise for the XY coordinates in Zone 39 and Zone40 for the survey corners

After all the explanations and exercises, how do we know that our seismic are in the right locations?

Pointers;

(1) The 2D vintages should tie with each other. If in the block or project area have more than one vintage, e.g., 1970, 1988, 1997, 2001, then all the four vintages must tie with each other.
(2) The 2D lines should tie with the overlaying 3D survey(s).
(3) If there are any wells, they should be right on the 2D line and shot-point, or the designated INLINE and CROSSLINE, i.e., intersection.

See more in **VIII. Data Harmonization.**

Now, most G&G workstations are menu driven. So inputting CRS to define a new project or loading new dataset or reloading dataset, one should always remember to do the following, no excuse:

> *Source CRS:*   *where the original data are defined.*
>
> *Destination CRS:*   *where the data should finally reside.*

As the example given in **Figure IV-16**,

(1) If one wants to work in UTM Zone 40, and we have data (say Data-A) defined in UTM Zone 39 to work alongside, thus

Source CRS for Data-A: CRS Zone 39
Destination CRS: CRS Zone 40.

(2) Vice versa, if we want to work in UTM Zone 39 and we have data (say Data-B) defined in UTM Zone 40 to work alongside, thus

Source CRS for Data-B: CRS Zone 40
Destination CRS: CRS Zone 39

FURTHER READINGS

	Title	Author	Date	Website
1	Guidance Notes On the Use of Coordinate Systems In Data Management on the UKSC	UKOOA	Dec-99	www.databydesign. co.uk
2	User's Handbook On Datum Transformation Involving WG84	International Hydrographic Organization	July 2003 (3rd edition)	www.nima.mil
3	Intro to existing formats. Reasons for ch and the change process.	OGP	2012	www.ogp.org.uk
4	MultiFix5 User Manual	Fugro Intersite Ltd	2-Nov-06	www.eaglegeo.co.uk
5	What is the diff between WGS84 and NAD83?	Mircea Neacsu	Oct-08	www.uvm.edu/ glv/resource/ WGS84_NAD83.pdf
6	Map Projections: A Working Manual	John Parr Snyder	1987	www.pubs.er.usgs. gov/publication/ pp1395
7	Map Projections Editor	Landmark System	2003	
8	Map Projections	US Geological Society	28-Dec-00	www.usgs.gov
9	Surveying and Positioning Guidance: Notes 1, 3, and 16	OGP	Note 1 (2008) Notes 3 and 16 (2006)	www.info.ogp. org.uk/geodesy
10	World Geodetic System			www.en.wikipedia. org/wiki/World_ Geodetic_System

V – THE FLOW: DATA MANAGEMENT

Data Management flows are set processes to regulate good governance to protect our data wherever they may be.

THE EIGHT GOLDEN RULES OF DATA MANAGEMENT

(1) Data collection, gathering, search
(2) Data verification, validation, cataloging, indexing, categorizing, reformat, scanning and vectorizing
(3) Data repository, input, load (manual/auto)
(4) Data verification, validation of loaded data
(5) Client, User participation
(6) Client, User approval
(7) Backup, restore of the loaded data
(8) Archive, storage upon project completion

PART I—ALGORITHM

DATA COLLECTION, GATHER, SEARCH

(1) Acquired data on CD, DVD, disk or USB in SEGY format which normally come with transmittal or note from the source describing the contents.

(2) Source can be the processing companies, block/permit partners or even your own company.

DATA VERIFICATION, VALIDATION, REFORMAT, SCANNING, VECTORIZING

(1) Media are labeled or indexed for notification, filing, storage or archive. The indexing are in accordance to industry standards.

(2) Data with non-conformal format are re-formatted to suit the industry standard format. For example 'old' format SEGA, SEGB SEGC to reformat to SEGD.

(3) Data are scanned from hardcopy to digital set.

DATA INPUT, LOAD, REPOSITORY

(1) Perform SEGY analysis for seismic data especially the spectral range.

(2) Perform navigation data analysis (2D).

(3) Loading 8, 16, or 32b depending on the data density received.

(4) Check data coverage visually.

(5) Create cube for 3D.

(6) Visualize in 3D mode for both 2D and 3D.

(7) Create a databank for seismic information and data

(8) Data transcribed or tape copy from 'old' media to current media mode.

(9) Ensure that the seismic repository generate informations of the EBDCDIC, Binary and Trace headers

DATA VALIDATION, VERIFICATION OF THE REPOSITED DATA

(1) Create seismic attributes for first-pass data validation
(2) Check on the cartographic location
(3) For multiple surveys/vintages check for ties

CLIENT, USER PARTICIPATION

(1) Get "green light" or post-job approval from client/user for the good loading job, i.e. signature on the completion form.
(2) Do record down any job done for future references.

New software do have log files generated for every job performed which is cumbersome at times to go through or retrieve these informations.

But its worthwhile for future references.

DEPT HEAD OR TEAM-LEAD APPROVAL

(1) The approval must be from the Head of the department or the Team-lead.
(2) This is normally done by conducting a presentation of the work done, a meeting and followed by a report.

DATA BACKUPS RESTORES

(1) Backup the loaded seismic in the format of the software used.
(2) Even the backup in SEGY format will have variations depending on outfit that generate the format.

DATA ARCHIVE, DELETE

(1) Upon completion of the project, perform data cleaning, backup for archival, and delete the project(s) from the system.

(2) The decision is entirely from the users Head of Dept or the Team-Lead.

Now keep in mind that we shall limit ourselves to seismic data. Other subsurface data topics will be discussed in the subsequent volume(s).

We now go through the details of the flow so as to equip ourselves with the familiarization in the management aspects of the seismic data.

PART II—DETAILS

DATA COLLECTION, GATHER, SEARCH

Data are retrieved from source(s) and placed in the area of common accessibility.

Data collection, gathering, searching are categorized into the following:

WAYS TO COLLECT, GATHER, SEARCH FOR DATA

• PHYSICAL — MEDIA

Data are on tapes, disks, CD, DVD or USB and, not to forget, papers and films if need be. Usually, these papers/films have been scanned and put on DVDs. Have a meticulous check to ensure all receiving data have been scanned or digitized.

Also, tape transcription is now a norm to have data transferred from 'old' tape media to present mode of media.

• ELECTRONICS — DATA TRANSFER REMOTELY

Data are transferred from another location via FTP.

This will take a bit of time, so try running it during off-peak hours.

• FORMS/TEMPLATES

This method only carries few important details, e.g., survey information.

In whatever form, please do ensure the following:

(1) Take note of anything pertaining to the collections or searching or gathering and also the setbacks encountered.
(2) Always sign the transmittals and never put it off to a later time. As humans, we might forget it. If you are extremely busy, delegate the job professionally to someone else.
(3) Also, handle these data with care and apply HSE procedures at all instances.
(4) Place these data in a safe but accessible area for further processes.

Now, what can be the worst scenarios?

Data not found?

So steps to be taken:

(1) Recheck request.
(2) Recheck whether data exist.

(3) For internal dataset, look in "strange" places, e.g., old warehouses.

(4) For partners, operating companies, service companies, please remind them of the contract or written agreement pertaining to data delivery in the MOU, LOI, …

SOURCES OF DATA

• PARTNERS

(1) Partners will provide all required information as per contract agreement.

(2) The receiving party should be well versed on the contents received.

For easy communication, it's better to furnish the partners with a template form of your data needs. This way, they can prepare the data to comply with your company requests.

Template forms are information sheets designed to capture key attributes e.g.

1	Type of surveys (2D, 3D, 4D)	8	3D inline & crossline increment
2	Environment of survey (onshore, offshore)	9	2D shot point interval
3	Cartography Reference System – CRS	10	2D shot-point – trace ratio
4	Survey extents	11	Acquisition company
5	Survey size	12	Processing company
6	Survey length	13	Operating company
7	3D inline & crossline interval (3D bin size)	14	…

• SERVICE COMPANIES

(1) Data acquisition companies through marine or land seismic surveys.
(2) Processing and imaging companies through processes that make the data interpretable to the clients.
(3) Special processing companies to generate seismic attributes e.g. inversion.

These companies (or contractors as we address them) will provide their clients with SEGD format, i.e., field tapes (unprocessed seismic) and SEGY, i.e., for the processed seismic.

Prior to SEGD format, field tapes come in the following format: SEGA, SEGB, and SEGC.

• OPERATING COMPANIES

These are petroleum companies that have license to work in blocks or areas in a particular region within a country of operation. The term is known as "farm-in."

As usual, their main partners is the state-owned oil company plus one or two or three other petroleum companies that have stakes or shares in the particular block or area.

The operator(s), as they are called, will take the lead in all activities but prior approvals from shareholding companies or block partners are required.

If you are in this outfit, then it is your prerogative to provide the seismic data (SEGY format) to the other companies.

Otherwise, you should collect data from the operator(s) in SEGY format.

These are companies that sell seismic data to the public, especially the oil & gas companies that intends to 'farm-in' into the area of interest.

They will acquire this data after an agreement with the authorities of the country concerned.

So if your company is involved in purchasing of the seismic data, do whatever necessary to safeguard your company's investment, which in turn is safeguarding your job, i.e.

1	Check the package	5	Get users to visualize the seismic
2	Scan the data	6	Get approval
3	Load the seismic ASAP	7	Backup the loaded seismic
4	Validate the loaded data	8	And last but not least, data archive and storage

At times old dataset on papers are thoroughly check and even perform a quick interpretion to generate a quick contour map in time dormain.

• OLD ARCHIVES

There are bound to be data stored away somewhere in premises, e.g., storerooms or warehouses.

It is imperative to have these data loaded in the systems.

This is the fun part, where you go through these "old" dataset normally on 9-track tapes, folded seismic papers, etc., etc. in the warehouse or storage rooms, and hopefully, they are regularly maintained.

If not, "wish" for the followings:

(1) These facilities are not water-logged or damp on the inside.
(2) The labels on the tapes are still readable.
(3) Paper media are still intact and not changing colors.
(4) There are no poisonous critters around.
(5) Someone still have the keys to these facilities.

- ## OLD MEDIA

Check all the old 9-track tapes. Rest assured that some data backed-up or archived may need reloading. This is especially true of dataset during the 8-bit era.

- ## INTERNET

The internet is another form of source giving us information of what data we should have but NOT available in our systems in other words 'in our safekeeping'.

As every bit of information is very valuable, so why *not* pursue on these missing data.

- ## REPORTS

No one can do without these. One can have lodes of data, but without reports is "*like one maneuvering in the dark.*"

With technology, one can now load reports plus other hardcopy documents directly into the database through scanning.

They are also an important source of navigation data on papers for old 2D lines.

Using the utility "File → Save as Other" in **Adobe Acrobat XI Pro** one can convert tables in pdf-format into MS Excel format.

Performed double checks on previous inputs in the database, especially 3D surveys parameters.

DATA VERIFICATION, IDENTIFICATION, TRANSCRIPTION, REFORMAT

Upon receiving the data, verify that this is the dataset requested/required.

CHECK THE TRANSMITTALS

This is the usual procedure for processing contractors to notify the clients of the dataset the clients are getting.

It can be fast-track, post-stack, angle-stack, avo, pre-stack, inversion, and other types of dataset in SEGY.

See **Appendix F: Seismic type** on page 177 for types of processed seismic one might receive.

Likewise, check for field tapes in SEGD format. These will normally come in cartons and will quickly be sent to the storage depot for safekeeping.

On the clients side, no one bothers to check the contents of the SEGD format because it needs a special kind of software to read these formatted dataset. Normallly these type of dataset are readable ONLY by processing software. As we speak there are 'souls' that have written free software to read these dataset.

Also the medium these dataset were transcribed onto are no more available in the market including the machine to read them.

Luckily most of the clients have embarked (and still does) on a tape-transcription project to have the dataset transcribed from the 'old' media to be onto the latest media i.e. the 1Tb or 2Tb or 4Tb hard-drive.

Some clients have these handled by appointed data storage companies or even by the processing contractors themselves.

NOTES ACCOMPANYING THE DATASET
(TO ELABORATE IN DETAIL)

These notes are usually from:

(1) Partner companies operating in the same block/acreage
(2) Operators from adjacent blocks. Data straddles across into each other blocks, and so through 'data exchange', all parties are in access of each other dataset.
(3) Processing companies which usually have the tendency to provide details of the processed data
(4) Departments or sister companies working on the same dataset for different projects, e.g., one company working on regional while another company working on development. Normally, in this case, they should have the same database but due to data confidentiality to other partners' outfit, only one copy of the same seismic data may be routed all over.

LABELS ON THE MEDIA

(1) Normally, the dataset comes from within the company themselves, from its datacenter.
(2) Backups/archives to be restored

As usual, read the label on the media, unless it's USB pendrive.

If none on ythe previous page applies, then check the contents, which needs special software and equipment to read the dataset.

CHECKING THE CONTENTS

(1) This can prove quite difficult for old media, e.g., ½" tape (9-track), ¼" floppy or 8" floppy disk.
(2) You probably have to assemble a PDP/HP tape deck for the ½" tape.
(3) For the ¼" floppy we have to get an external drive or an old laptop or desktop.

(4) For the 8" floppy, probably you need to search high and low for the reader or machine (Tips: old Wang Microcomputer or others . . .).

(5) For the floppies, they not only contain ASCII files but data in the format generated by the software used.

(6) It's always better to check first, i.e., read the media involved than wishing later on "I should have read the media first."

DATA INPUT/LOAD

Prior to any loading, please run an amplitude scan to visualize the amplitude dynamic range. The data can be stored in 32-bit format but amplitude range less than ±30000. So in this particular case, it is better to load the data in 16-bit. This will save the storage space by half the original size.

Example, the 32-bit dataset is twice the size of the 16-bit dataset which in turn is twice the size of the 8-bit dataset.

"**Never ever load any data blindly.**"

For a new dataset, the software can now load automatically by detecting the right and appropriate byte locations. Be careful about the CRS(Cartographic/Coordinate Reference System).

During loading, do check for the XY coordinate's scalar. At times, default is in decimeter rather than meter; thus, the coordinates' values are down by a factor of 10. This can result in surveys (or wells) to be displayed in the "wrong" location.

For 3D			
i	INLINE	(byte – 185)	4 – byte
ii	XLINE	(byte – 189)	4 – byte
iii	X-COORD	(byte – 73)	4 – byte
iv	Y-COORD	(byte – 77)	4 – byte
For 2D			
i	SP	(byte – 9)	4 – byte
ii	TRACE/CDP	(byte – 21)	4 – byte
iii	X-COORD	(byte – 73)	4 – byte
iv	Y-COORD	(byte – 77)	4 – byte

So why go through all these steps?

Reasons:

(1) These are for 'old' seismic data in SEGY format
(2) To duly understand the real concept of seismic data loading, check if it might be from the partners (SEGYOUT backup) or from the archives.
(3) If from partners, the SEGYOUT dataset are always customize. So check thoroughly the bytes locations for key parameters needed for the loading.

PERFORMING NAVIGATION DATA ANALYSIS (2D)

(1) This is normally done if the XY coordinates are *not* presence in the trace header.
(2) As discussed in detail earlier in **IV. Coordinate Reference System** on page 61, the format normally is of UKOOA-84 (old) to UKOOA-91 (latest).
(3) The simplest format one can receive is in ASCII e.g. below:

SP No.	X	Y

70

(4) Then we have to deal with the SP – CDP (Shotpoint – Common Depth Point) relationship. That's the reason why it is necessary to have the XY in the trace. SEGY data all have XY in the trace header at byte location 73 (X) and location 77 (Y). At times X (byte 181) and Y (byte 185).

(5) If we have no clue to what is the SP–TR (Shotpoint – Trace) relationship, then check the SP range (e.g., 1 – 800) then apply TR #1 (trace number 1) to the first SP then TR #800 (trace number 800) to the last SP. Thus the ratio here 1:1.

> *Note:*
>
> *Upon receiving SEGY output from partners, always request them for the CRS parameters they have defined for loading their seismic data.*
>
> *These parameters are then input in our own system and used as SOURCE CRS.*

CREATE PROJECT OR SURVEYS, DEPENDING ON THE DATA

> *A seismic project is defined as an acreage covering surface zones of interest in a block or "farm-in" area.*
>
> A seismic project can have a single seismic survey or multiple seismic surveys—2D, 3D, or both. See *Figure III-4* in *III. Seismic Surveys* on page *43*.

(1) For a new project, create the project first before creating a survey or surveys be it 2D or 3D or both.

(2) Try not to create survey ahead of receiving data because:

- The survey information in the media might not match the survey created.

- The data might be received on a later date say, e.g., a month or two [2] but the created survey is already deceiving users as to its presence.

You can bet on it that your phone (or HP) will start ringing at quite regular intervals.

And we do want to keep our database clean.

It is commendable to scribble our survey on a piece of paper or note book to visualize how the 3D survey will appear in the workstation. Example see **Figure VII-4** in **VII. Seismic Data Loading**.

LOADING 8, 16, OR 32B, DEPENDING ON THE DATA DENSITY RECEIVED

Normally, the seismic data received in the following data bit-format:

Bit – format	Comments
32b float/integer	New dataset
8b:16b:32b float/integer	Backup dataset
8b float/integer	'Old' dataset pre-1990s

Table V-1: Data bit-format

> *One should NOT forget (or even confuse) the difference between* ***data-storage formats*** *and* ***data-bit formats***.
>
> ***Data storage format*** *is the way data is stored in the media, whereas* ***data-bit format*** *is how the data are to be displayed, i.e., the dynamic amplitude range.*

In fact, new software releases are using SEGY seismic direct for interpretation in 32-bit floating.

Some software go to the extent of compressing the SEGY seismic for speed and space optimization. This is performed knowing that the amplitude range is within the 16-bit or 8-bit values. Refer back to **VI. Segy Header Analysis**.

CHECK DATA COVERAGE VISUALLY

(1) Create cube for 3D.
(2) Visualize in 3D mode for both 2D and 3D

It is a good practice to also input data in 3D visualization mode.

All interpretation packages purchased have this embedded feature.

3D mode:

(1) Gives a better picture of your good work in loading seismic
(2) Gives a better amplitude display
(3) Gives a better geophysical/geological sense in the seismic tie or misties between the 2D line and 3D surveys.

DATA VALIDATION (FOR CORRECTIONS)

After the loading, prior to "sitting" down with the user(s), ensure that the loading is perfect no hiccups;

(1) Survey parameters for 3D are correct.
(2) 2D and/or 3D are loaded with the correct CRS.
(3) The seismic are with the correct amplitude scaling.
(4) In loading high resolution (hi-res), ensure that the sample rate use in loading is the same as the 3D or 2D seismic loaded. Normally, hi-res seismic have a 1ms sample rate.

At this stage, the clients/users should not be in the picture – this is a must.

Do run a few seismic attributes to ensure the validity of the seismic data loaded. Attributes can be in the form of phase, frequency, and others. (Look for topics in the Internet on seismic characterization for details)

This will ensure that time has been saved by proper loading and mind us that 'time is money'.

Do record down any job done for future references even though software do have log files which are usually cumbersome to decipher.

USER PARTICIPATION

This is the part where user(s) will be eager and jubilated to visualize the data we loaded.

Always prepare the survey and data summary sheet;

3D SURVEY INFORMATION SHEET

i	Inline range	vii	Sample rate
ii	Crossline range	viii	Bit loaded
iii	Time range	ix	Any scaling
iv	Depth range	x	Any problems encountered
v	Inline bin size	xi	Full details of the CRS applied
vi	Crossline bin size	xii	Elevation Datum (onshore)

2D LINES INFORMATION SHEET

i	Vintage	vii	Sample rate
ii	No. of lines loaded	viii	Bit loaded
iii	Time range	ix	Any scaling
iv	Depth range	x	Any problems encountered
v	Shot interval	xi	Full details of the CRS applied
vi	SP – TR ratio	xii	Elevation Datum (onshore)

When the clients/users have the summary sheet (s), they now have total confidence in you.

> *TO DO WITHOUT FAIL*
>
> *Get the "green light" from the user for the good loading job, i.e. a signature on the completion form will suffice.*

APPROVAL

"It's not over until it's over" unless we finally secure the approval from the Head of the Department or the Team – Lead.

Upon approval means that the data are ready to be worked upon or interpreted.

Again, ensure that the acceptance form is signed.

It's a good practice to conduct a short meeting or presentation on the job done and sent a short report of the loading job to all parties involved so that everyone concerned is kept in the "loop." Include also any image snapshots taken during the loading and verification.

This will ensure that the clients/users are aware what problems have been encountered and the solutions during the processes prior to the approval.

BACKUP/RESTORE

To ensure data integrity and safety, quickly perform the backup of the seismic data loaded ASAP. It is a very good practise to perform immediately after the loading stage prior to the session with the clients/users, as at times it takes a few days before the clients/users have time for us.

The seismic loaded is in the format of the software platform used.

> *This is seldom or "never" done – run a test restore project to confirm that the backup designed is 100% functional.*

This is the first of a series of backups that will be scheduled until the end of the project.

It will normally be in the following sequence known as "snapshots" on a NETAPPS system:

(1) Every quarter of an hour (incremental)
(2) Nightly (incremental)
(3) Weekly (incremental)
(4) Monthly (complete backup)
(5) Yearly (complete backup)

Incremental backup means only the files created or modified are backed-up. Normally, horizons and other meta-files are included in this category.

The original seismic volumes loaded should be backed-up only once after the loading.

Other seismic attributes volumes are only backed-up after they are deemed finalized by the users.

Total backup means every file or folder under the project is backed-up including seismic volumes.

DATA ARCHIVE, DELETE

This is done after a project closure, i.e., the project has been decommissioned. Make sure that the project is cleaned before archiving is performed. See **IX. Backup, Archive and Restore**.

Archiving can be performed either on the hard drive or on external media like LTO/DLT. Upon ensuring that the project is totally archived then it can be removed or deleted from the system.

DATA SECURITY

What about Data Security?

This is a million-dollar question, and let us be presumptuous about these.

(1) This has to be worked out with the IT infrastructure team to ensure that no data can be accessed through the network.
(2) Only the data management team can input and output SEGY seismic data or restore the backups.
(3) No users are allowed to load/output any seismic data. If anything goes wrong, the accountability or onus is on you! Even if they are the only friends you have in the entire galaxy or universe. Or better still, de-activate all menus pertaining to SEGY input/output.
(4) Seismic attributes generation are the prerogative of the seismic interpreters (i.e. users) and they can generate as many as they want as long as the un-used ones are deleted (done only by data managers) within a limited timeframe.
(5) There are many more that can be listed but most diligently, be on your toes . . . yes, you data managers!

FURTHER READINGS

1	Refer to all Data Management manuals by G&G software vendors.
2	Also, refer to basic project management books as some of the flows runs parallel to the subsurface data management routines.

VI – SEGY HEADER ANALYSIS

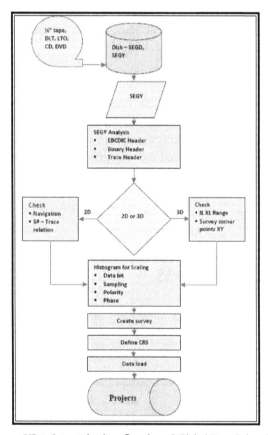

Figure VI-1: Seismic loading flowchart ©Global Data Subsurface

Figure **VI-1** shows a flowchart on which both this chapter and **VII. Seismic Data Loading** on page **129** will be based upon.

Algorithm:

(1) Read the data from tape (old media), DLTs, LTOs, CDs, DVDs, or direct access disk storage.

(2) Determine the format, i.e., SEGA, SEGB, SEGC, SEGD, or SEGY. Processed seismic data are generated in SEGY format as the final standard output.

(3) When the SEGY is determined, check the three standard headers:

i	EBCDIC
ii	BINARY
iii	TRACE

(4) Check for which type of survey the SEGY data are generated;

2D	
1	the navigation
2	the SP–TR relationship for any available information.
3D	
4	the INLINE/XLINE ranges
5	the XY for the surveys four (4) corner points.

(5) Check the histogram for the seismic data which will furnish us with the amplitude ranges for the dataset. This will tell us the bit format of the data received.

Do not get confused between data-storage format and the data-bit format.

Data-storage format:

1. *The way the data are stored on the media.*

Data-bit format:

2. *Reflects the amplitude range of the data. See section on* **Data bit-format** *on page 117.*

As stated earlier, there are three headers:

(1) EBCDIC header (3200 bytes)
(2) BINARY header (400 bytes)
(3) TRACE header (240 bytes)

And this is a standard SEGY format used throughout the industry for processed seismic data.

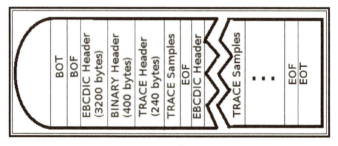

Figure VI-2: Tape format—SEGY

SEGY FORMAT

(1) A 3600-byte reel identification header:

- The first part is the **3200 bytes** consisting of an ASCII header block i.e. 40 lines and 80 characters or bytes per line.
- The second part is the **400-byte** binary header block.
- Both headers include information specific to the line and reel number, respectively.

(2) The trace data block follows the reel identification header. The first **240 bytes** of each trace block is the binary trace identification header.

(3) The seismic data samples follow the trace identification header.

EBCDIC HEADER

Figure VI-3: Example of 3D survey SEGY—EBCDIC header

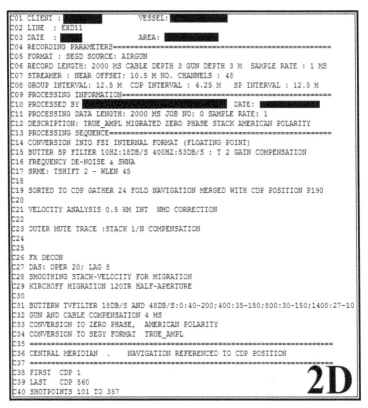

```
C01 CLIENT :  ███████        VESSEL: ███████████
C02 LINE   : EXD11
C03 DATE   : ████           AREA: ███████████
C04 RECORDING PARAMETERS===================================================
C05 FORMAT : SEGD SOURCE: AIRGUN
C06 RECORD LENGTH: 2000 MS CABLE DEPTH 3 GUN DEPTH 3 M  SAMPLE RATE : 1 MS
C07 STREAMER : NEAR OFFSET: 10.5 M NO. CHANNELS : 48
C08 GROUP INTERVAL: 12.5 M  CDP INTERVAL : 6.25 M   SP INTERVAL : 12.5 M
C09 PROCESSING INFORMATION===================================================
C10 PROCESSED BY ███████████████████████       DATE: ████████████
C11 PROCESSING DATA LENGTH: 2000 MS JOB NO: 0 SAMPLE RATE: 1
C12 DESCRIPTION: TRUE_AMPL MIGRATED ZERO PHASE STACK AMERICAN POLARITY
C13 PROCESSING SEQUENCE=====================================================
C14 CONVERSION INTO FSI INTERNAL FORMAT (FLOATING POINT)
C15 BUTTER BP FILTER 10HZ:18DB/S 400HZ:53DB/S : T 2 GAIN COMPENSATION
C16 FREQUENCY DE-NOISE & SWNA
C17 SRME: TSHIFT 2 - WLEN 45
C18
C19 SORTED TO CDP GATHER 24 FOLD NAVIGATION MERGED WITH CDP POSITION P190
C20
C21 VELOCITY ANALYSIS 0.5 KM INT  NMO CORRECTION
C22
C23 OUTER MUTE TRACE :STACK 1/N COMPENSATION
C24
C25
C26 FX DECON
C27 DAS: OPER 20; LAG 8
C28 SMOOTHING STACK-VELOCITY FOR MIGRATION
C29 KIRCHOFF MIGRATION 120TR HALF-APERTURE
C30
C31 BUTTERW TVFILTER 18DB/S AND 48DB/S:0:40-200;400:35-180;800:30-150;1400:27-10
C32 GUN AND CABLE COMPENSATION 4 MS
C33 CONVERSION TO ZERO PHASE,  AMERICAN POLARITY
C34 CONVERSION TO SEGY FORMAT  TRUE_AMPL
C35 =====================================================================
C36 CENTRAL MERIDIAN  .   NAVIGATION REFERENCED TO CDP POSITION
C37 =====================================================================
C38 FIRST  CDP 1
C39 LAST   CDP 560                                            2D
C40 SHOTPOINTS 101 TO 357
```

Figure VI-4: Example of 2D survey SEGY—EBCDIC header

(1) 80 characters on each line of 40 and that makes 3200 bytes.

(2) Contains information for project outline, navigation, and processing sequence.

(3) What to look for?

Based on the example in **Figures VI-3** and **VI-4**

	Information	2D	3D
1	Seismic types, e.g., STACK, MIG, PRESTACK Time or Depth MIGRATION	TRUE AMPLITUE MIGRATION	MIGRATION
2	Depth	Time (ms)	Time (ms)
3	Polarity – NORMAL or REVERSE6	REVERSE (SEGY polarity)	REVERSE
4	Phase – MIN or ZERO.	ZERO	ZERO
5	Sampling rate – 1ms, 2ms or 4ms.	1ms	4ms
6	Record length – 2000ms, 2500ms, 3000ms, 4000ms, 5000ms, 10000ms, etc.	2000ms	5000ms
7	INLINE ranges and/ or bytes location.		INLINE BYTE 189 – 192
8	XLINE ranges and/ or bytes location.		XLINE (CDP) BYTE 21 – 24
9	LINENAME	EXD11	1143
10	SHOTPOINT ranges and/or bytes location for the SHOTPOINT.	101 – 357	
11	SHOTPOINT ranges and/or bytes location for the SHOTPOINT.	1 – 560	
12	3D Survey outlines, i.e., the four (4) corner points, each point having XY and/or bytes location for X, Y coordinates.		In this example, no information
13	CRS information – Datum: Projection: UTM Zone: CM:	In this example, no information	In this example, no information
14	Elevation Datum (onshore)	In this example, no information	In this example, no information

Table IV-1: Information from SEGY EBCDIC header for 2D and 3D surveys

Alternatively, for Depth-seismic, it can be Z in meters or feet.

BINARY HEADER

3201	0	Job identification number
3205	1143	Line number
3209	0	Reel number
3213	1150	Number of data traces per ensemble
3215	0	Number of auxiliary traces per ensemble
3217	4000	Sample interval in microseconds (ms)
3219	4000	Sample interval in microseconds (ms) of original field recording
3221	1252	Number of samples per data trace
3223	1252	Number of samples per data trace for original field recording
3225	1	Data sample format code 1 = 4-byte IBM floating-point 2 = 4-byte i...
3227	1150	Ensemble fold - The expected number of data traces per trace ensemble
3229	0	Trace sorting code (i.e. type of ensemble)
3231	0	Vertical sum code
3233	0	Sweep frequency at start (Hz)
3235	0	Sweep frequency at end (Hz)
3237	0	Sweep length (ms)
3239	0	Sweep type code
3241	0	Trace number of sweep channel
3243	0	Sweep trace taper length in milliseconds at start if tapered
3245	0	Sweep trace taper length in milliseconds at end
3247	0	Taper type
3249	0	Correlated data traces
3251	0	Binary gain recovered
3253	0	Amplitude recovery method
3255	1	Measurement system
3257	0	Impulse signal polarity
3259	0	Vibratory polarity code
3261	434747334...	* Unassigned bytes *
3501	0	SEG Y Format Revision Number
3503	0	Fixed length trace flag
3505	0	Number of 3200-byte, Extended Textual File Headers
3507	000000000...	* Unassigned bytes *

3D Binary Hdr

Figure VI-5: Example of 3D survey SEGY—binary header

Value	Description	Bytes
1	Job identification number	1- 4
11	* Line number	5- 8
1	* Reel number	9- 12
48	* # data traces per record	13- 14
0	* # aux traces per record	15- 16
1000	* Sample interval (microseconds) for reel	17- 18
0	Sample interval (microseconds) for field	19- 20
2000	* Number samples per data trace for reel	21- 22
0	Number samples per data trace for field	23- 24
1	* Data sample format code	25- 26
24	* CDP fold	27- 28
4	* Trace sorting code	29- 30
1	Vertical sum code	31- 32
0	Sweep frequency at start	33- 34
0	Sweep frequency at end	35- 36
0	Sweep length (milliseconds)	37- 38
0	Sweep type code	39- 40
0	Trace number of sweep channel	41- 42
0	Sweep trace taper length at start (ms)	43- 44
0	Sweep trace taper length at end (ms)	45- 46
0	Taper type	47- 48
0	Correlated data traces	49- 50
0	Binary gain recovered	51- 52
0	Amplitude recovery method	53- 54
1	Measurement system (1-m / 2-feet)	55- 56
0	Impulse signal	57- 58
0	Vibratory polarity code	59- 60
0	- SSC Co SEG-Y samples number	63- 66
0.0	SEG-Y Rev	301-302
0	Fixed trace flag	303-304
0	Number of Extended Textual Headers	305-304

2D Binary Hdr

Figure VI-6: Example of 2D survey SEGY—binary header

Information	2D	3D
Line number	11	1143
Sampling rate	1000µs (1ms)	4000µs(4ms)
No. of samples per trace	2000	1252

Table VI-2: Information from SEGY binary header for surveys 2D and 3D

TRACE HEADER

Name	Byte	Value	Description
TRACENO	1	1	Trace sequence number within line
	5	1143	Trace sequence number within reel
FFID	9	3600183	Original field record number
CHAN	13	721	Trace sequence number within field record
SOURCE	17	64619482	Energy source point number
CDP	21	1150	CDP ensemble number
SEQNO	25	0	Trace sequence number within CDP ensemble
TRC_TYPE	29	1	Trace identification code
STACKCNT	31	15	Number of vertically summed traces
TRFOLD	33	0	Number of horizontally stacked traced
	35	1	Data use (1 = production, 2 = test)
OFFSET	37	731	Distance from source point to receiver group
REC_ELEV	41	64619482	Receiver group elevation
SOU_ELEV	45	344	Surface elevation at source
DEPTH	49	60359642	Source depth below surface
REC_DATUM	53	1	Datum elevation at receiver group
SOU_DATUM	57	2857500	Datum elevation at source
SOU_H2OD	61	64619482	Water depth at source
REC_H2OD	65	1404	Water depth at receiver group
	69	0	Scalar for elevations and depths
	71	60	Scalar for coordinates
SOU_X	73	209880	X source coordinate
SOU_Y	77	9294350	Y source coordinate
REC_X	81	209149	X receiver group coordinate
REC_Y	85	9294350	Y receiver group coordinate
	89	21	Coordinate units (1 - meters or feet, 2 - arc seconds)
	91	-4292	Weathering velocity
	93	0	Subweathering velocity
UPHOLE	95	1925	Uphole time at source
REC_UPHOLE	97	0	Uphole time at receiver group
SOU_STAT	99	0	Source static correction
REC_STAT	101	77	Receiver group static correction
TOT_STAT	103	1	Total static applied
	105	3	Lag time between end of header and time break in ms
	107	12908	Lag time between time break and shot in ms
	109	0	Lag time beteen shot and recording start in ms
TLIVE_S	111	12	Start of mute time
TFULL_S	113	44	End of mute time
NUMSMP	115	1252	Number of samples in this trace
DT	117	4000	Sample interval of this trace in microseconds
IGAIN	119	0	Field instrument gain type code
PREAMP	121	942	Instrument gain constant
EARLYG	123	700	Intrument early gain in dB
COR_FLAG	125	1398	Correlated (1 - no / 2 - yes)
SWEEPFREQSTART	127	1176	Sweep frequency at start
SWEEPFREQEND	129	1331	Sweep fequency at end
SWEEPLEN	131	1441	Sweep length in ms
SWEEPTYPE	133	1173	Sweep type code (1 - linear, 2 - parabolic, 3 - exponential, 4 - other)
SWEEPTAPSTART	135	1254	Sweep taper trace length at start in ms
SWEEPTAPEND	137	1010	Sweep taper trace length at end in ms
SWEEPTAPCODE	139	1092	Taper type code (1 - linear, 2 - cosine squared. 3 - other)

3D Trace Hdr

(Continued)

AAXFILT	141	990	Alias filter frequency
AAXSLOP	143	993	Alias filter slope
FREQXN	145	988	Notch filter frequency
FXNSLOP	147	988	Notch filter slope
FREQXL	149	12	Low cut frequency
FREQXH	151	-11507	High cut frequency
FXLSLOP	153	986	Low cut slope
FXHSLOP	155	986	High cut slope
YEAR	157	985	Year data recorded
DAY	159	985	Day of year
HOUR	161	985	Hour of day (24-hour clock)
MINUTE	163	985	Minute of hour
SECOND	165	985	Second of minute
	167	984	Time basis (1 - local, 2 - GMT, 3 - other)
	169	985	Trace weighting factor for fixed-point format data
	171	985	Geophone group number of roll switch position one
	173	984	Geophone group number of first trace of original field record
	175	984	Geophone group number of last trace of original field record
	177	986	Gap size (total number of groups dropped)
	179	986	Overtravel associated with taper (1 - down/behind, 2 - up/ahead)
CDP_X	181	3630185	X coordinate of ensemble (CDP)
CDP_Y	185	22806528	Y coordinate of ensemble (CDP)
ILINE_NO	189	1143	Inline number
XLINE_NO	193	1448	Xline number
	197	-1305	Shotpoint number
	201	0	Scalar to be applied to the shotpoint number
	203	2490	Trace value measurement unit
	205	141	Transduction Constant
	211	0	Transduction Units
	213	0	Device Trace Identifier
	215	0	Scalar to be applied to times specified in Trace Header bytes 94-113
	217	0	Source Type/Orientation
	219	1143	Source Energy Direction
	225	0	Source Measurement
	231	324	Source Measurement Units
	233	0001AEBD0...	* Unassigned — For optional information *

3D Trace Hdr

Figure VI-7: Example of 3D survey SEGY—TRACE header

87

1	* Trace sequence number within line	1- 4
1	Trace sequence number within reel	5- 8
0	* FFID - Original field record number	9- 12
1	* Trace number within field record	13- 16
77	SP - Energy source point number	17- 20
1	CDP ensemble number	21- 24
0	Trace number	25- 28
1	* Trace identification code	29- 30
0	Number of vertically summed traces	31- 32
1	Number of horizontally stacked traces	33- 34
1	Data use (1-production, 2-test)	35- 36
598	Distance from source point to receiv grp	37- 40
0	Receiver group elevation	41- 44
0	Surface elevation at source	45- 48
0	Source depth below surface	49- 52
0	Datum elevation at receiver group	53- 56
0	Datum elevation at source	57- 60
342	Water depth at source	61- 64
0	Water depth at group	65- 68
-10	Scaler to all elevations & depths	69- 70
-100	Scaler to all coordinates	71- 72
0	Source X coordinate	73- 76
0	Source Y coordinate	77- 80
774	Group X coordinate	81- 84
-59800	Group Y coordinate	85- 88
1	Coordinate units (1-lenm/ft 2-secarc)	89- 90
0	Weathering velocity	91- 92
0	Subweathering velocity	93- 94
0	Uphole time at source	95- 96
0	Uphole time at group	97- 98
0	Source static correction	99-100
0	Group static correction	101-102
0	Total static applied	103-104
0	Lag time A	105-106
0	Lag time B	107-108
0	Delay Recording time	109-110

2D Trace Hdr

(Continued)

0	Mute time start	111-112
0	Mute time end	113-114
2000	* Number of samples in this trace	115-116
1000	* Sample interval in ms for this trace	117-118
0	Gain type of field instruments	119-120
0	Instrument gain	121-122
0	Instrument gain constant	123-124
0	Correlated (1-yes / 2-no)	125-126
0	Sweep frequency at start	127-128
0	Sweep frequency at end	129-130
0	Sweep lenth in ms	131-132
0	Sweep type 1-lin,2-parabol,2-exp,4-ohter	133-134
0	Sweep trace taper length at start in ms	135-136
0	Sweep trace taper length at end in ms	137-138
0	Taper type 1-lin,2-cos2,3-other	139-140
0	Alias filter frequency, if used	141-142
0	Alias filter slope	143-144
0	Low cut frequency, if used	149-150
0	High cut frequency, if used	151-152
0	Low cut slope	153-154
0	High cut slope	155-156
2011	Year data recorded	157-158
253	Day of year	159-160
2	Hour of day	161-162
20	Minute of hour	163-164
35	Second of minute	165-166
2	Time basis code 1-local,2-GMT,3-other	167-168
0	Trace weighting factor	169-170
0	Geophone group number of roll sw pos 1	171-172
0	Geophone group number of trace # 1	173-174
0	Geophone group number of last trace	175-176
0	Gap size (total # of groups dropped)	177-178
0	Overtravel assoc w taper of beg/end line	179-180
0	+ CDP X	181-184
1	+ CDP Y	185-188
0	+ Inline Number	189-192
19535130	+ Clossline Number	193-196
928277565	+ Shot Point Number	197-200
0	+ Shot Point Scalar	201-202
0	+ Trace value measurement unit	203-204

2D Trace Hdr

Figure VI-8: Example of 2D survey SEGY: TRACE Header

Info	2D		3D	
	Byte	Values	Byte	Values
Inline			189 – 192	1143
Crossline			193 – 196	1448
CDP	21 – 24	1	21 – 24	1150
No. of samples per trace	115 – 116	2000	115 – 116	1252
Sample rate	117 – 118	1000us	117 – 118	4000us
X-coord	193 – 196	19535130dm	181 – 184	3630185cm
Y-coord	197 – 200	928277565dm	185 – 188	22806528cm

Table VI-3: Information from SEGY trace header for surveys 2D and 3D

Always used the XY coordinates from the TRACE header in determining the position of the SP or CDP rather than the XY – range information provided in the EBCDIC. header.

The information in the EBCDIC header might be the planned survey, *not* the final survey.

Alternatively, check the survey final coordinates information either in the Acquisition report or the Processing report.

SURVEYS

2D SEISMIC SURVEY

i	Linename (LN)	vii	Sample rate
ii	Shot- Linename point (SP)	viii	Data format
iii	Trace/CDP	ix	Polarity
iv	XY–easting & northing	x	Phase mode
v	Lat & Lon	xi	Elevation Datum
vi	Record length		

LINE NAME

(1) Normally denoted in the EBCDIC header
(2) At times is registered in the BINARY header
(3) "Never?" been registered in the TRACE header

SHOT-POINT

(1) Normally in the TRACE header.
(2) In the EBCDIC header, only the range is shown, e.g., SP 201–900.
(3) Also, this can be shown in the BINARY header as SP range.

The above information should be in both the EBCDIC header and the TRACE header. If the information is in the TRACE header *only*, then the loading of the relationship is accomplished.

But if the header is in EBCDIC header *only* or on some transmittal, then we should use the mathematical calculation for CDP–SP relation.

Take note of the Shotpoint interval which is normally 6.25, 12.5 & 25m. Any values than these e.g. 6.10, 11.95, 24.65 will make the line shorter than the original.

So checked and used the XY in the trace header if possible if you have doubt in the navigation files.

TRACE (CDP)–SP RELATION

See Table VI-4 for example.

Trace/CDP Range	SP Range	Relation CDP:SP
1–100	101–200	1 : 1
1–101	101–150	2 : 1
1–104	101–125	4 : 1

Table VI-4: Examples of CDP–SP relationship

[A "quick" get around if *no* information is available including the paper section, is to load 1:1 ratio]

> *Final value (SP) = ([Input Value*Multiplier] + Addition)/Divisor*

E.g. let's take **Table VI-5** and we want to use the first column –Trace, to get the result of the fifth column – SP.

- ## 1:1 RATIO

Trace (input value)	*	+	/	SP (final value)
1	1	100	1	101
2	1	100	1	102
3	1	100	1	103
… 101	1	100	1	201

Table VI-5: CDP–SP, 1 to 1 ratio

- ## 2:1 RATIO

Trace (Input value)	*	+	/	SP (Final value)
1	1	201	2	101
2	1	201	2	101.5
3	1	201	2	102
4	1	201	2	102.5
5	1	201	2	103
… 101	1	201	2	151

Table VI-6: CDP–SP, 2 to 1 ratio

- ## 5:1 RATIO

Trace (Input value)	*	+	/	SP (Final value)
1	1	504	5	101
2	1	504	5	

3	1	504	5	
4	1	504	5	
... 101	1	504	5	121

Table VI-7: CDP–SP, 5 to 1 ratio

> - *Multiply the SP by the value of the DIVISOR.*
> - *The result minus the multiplicity of the TRACE and multiplier to get the ADDITION value.*

Another example;

• 7:1 RATIO

Trace (input value)	*	+	/	SP (final value)
1	1	706	7	101
2	1	706	7	
3	1	706	7	
...				
8	1	706	7	102
...				
15	1	706	7	103
...				
71	1	706	7	111
...				

Table VI-8: CDP–SP, 7 to 1 ratio

XY – EASTING AND NORTHING

We see these values in the trace headers: byte locations 73 (X) and 77 (Y).

At times, we see X and Y at locations 81 and 85. These are group receiver XY.

And we load only from the byte locations **73** and **77**.

If XY is *not* in the standard SEGY byte locations **73 and 77,** then check at locations down below; **181** and **185** or **185** and **189.** The usual practise is to have the XY byte location indicated in the trace header.

Verify also that the XY is of the right scale, e.g., six-digit integer for X and seven-digit integer for Y. If XY have more than the intended digits, then XY values have to be scaled down. But please do check the values of the XY axes in the projection system map for reference.

If XY are not being indicated anywhere in the trace header, then they will be in a separate ASCII file normally in a UKOOA format.

For old dataset, the navigation data might be printed in the report or any other form of hardcopy.

If none, this is when the fun begins. Do not waste time "shedding sweat and tears"; do one of the following;

(1) Get the pseudo XY from the scaled map, i.e., start-of-line (SOL) and end-of-line (EOL).
(2) For an unscaled map, e.g., scanned map, the inaccuracy will be worse than one (1), but we still have a 2D project to work upon.
(3) Someone somehow has generated an ASCII file having SOL and EOL

But all of the above have another major setback for offshore acquisition.

The 2D lines acquired are not a near straight in traversed. Due to bad weather and swelling of the seas/oceans, the lines start to move from the actual traverse path in what they call "feathering."

The consultant on board might accept the diversity with a few degrees but at times have to accept to minimize downtime. Or the alternative is performing another reshoot of the line(s) in question.

Anyway, we now have the X and Y values to be contented with.

LATITUDE AND LONGITUDE

Seldom do we find LAT and LON values in any of the headers. If we were to find any, it should be in the EBCDIC header.

Normally, it is an indicative of the central meridian (e.g., 7°) in the coordinate reference systems used for the project or an indicative of the project area.

LAT/LON is in two formats:

(1) DMS (degree, minute, seconds)
(2) DD (degree in decimal)

RECORD LENGTH

The sample rate multiplied (×) by the number of samples in a trace.

(1) High resolution seismic 1500 – 2500ms.
(2) 4000, 5000, 6000ms.
(3) Seldom 6000ms in deep marine seismic program > 7000 – 20000ms.
(4) For depth-seismic, the record length can be between 10000m – 45000m.

Figure 6–9 is an example of various pseudo surveys with different seismic record length.

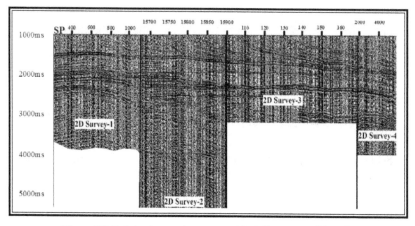

Figure VI-9: Seismic pseudo surveys with different record lengths

SAMPLE RATES

i	1 ms	iii	3 ms
ii	2 ms	iv	4 ms

From the *pseudo trace* in **Figure 6-12** below, the sampling rate **1ms** reflects more features than **2ms** or **4ms**, likewise with **2ms** as compared to **4ms**. **3ms** sample rate is still in use, but it's a rarity.

In brief:

1ms	Not used in normal seismic but in VSP [vertical seismic profiling] corridor stacks
2ms	High precision survey hazard survey
3ms	Rarely output
4ms	Normal output

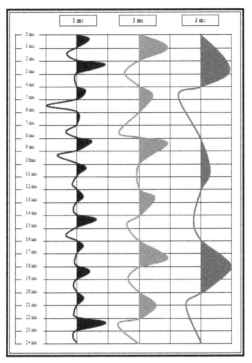

Figure VI-10: Example of sampling rates @amsar58

Offshore surveys

- *Seismic record usually starts from 0ms until the end of record processed.*

Onshore surveys

- *From 0ms OR*

- *From the actual processed data (minus [-] a value, e.g., -125 m, -200 m or -500 m). These values are what are known as survey datum or elevation datum.*

For details, refer to **VII. Seismic Data loading**.

DATA FORMAT

> ➤ Floating point or integer

• DATA STORAGE – FORMAT

(1) Check the SEGY headers normally in the TRACE header but can be registered in the EBCDIC header.
(2) Standard types:

i	IBM floating	iv	16-bit integer
ii	IEEE	v	32-bit integer
iii	8-bit integer		

• DATA BIT – FORMAT OR SAMPLE FORMAT

(1) 8-bit (old systems and old vintages).
(2) 16-bit (usual format for interpretation and optimal for amplitude extraction and velocity loading).
(3) 32-bit (seldom used as it takes twice as much disk space as 16-bit data but good for detailed study on amplitudes).

➤ 8-BIT INTEGER

2^8= **256** (unsigned)

Due to reflectivity amplitudes, = ±128 (signed)

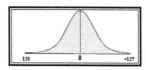

Figure VI-11: Histogram for 8-bit data

➤ 16-BIT INTEGER

2^{16}= **65536** (unsigned)

Due to reflectivity amplitudes, = ±32768 (signed)

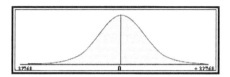

Figure VI-12: Histogram for 16-bit data

➢ 32-BIT INTEGER

2^{32}= **4294967296** (unsigned)

Due to reflectivity amplitudes, = ±2147483648 (signed)

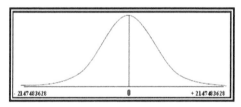

Figure VI-13: Histogram for 32-bit data

➢ 64-BIT INTEGER

= 18,446,744,073,709,551,615 (unsigned)

Due to reflectivity amplitudes,
= ±9,223,372,036,854,775,808 (signed)

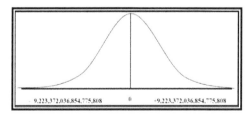

Figure VI-14: Histogram for 64-bit data

POLARITY

Polarity is a representation of the seismic amplitudes on either side of the positive/negative scale, depending on the acoustic impedance at the formation boundaries.

And these can be applied to the both the min/zero phases.

See **Figure 6-15**. The figure shows two pseudo traces side by side, reverse polarity, and normal polarity.

Reverse Polarity	It's also known as positive polarity—SEGY. Increase in impedance in the peak (black/ (+) value).
Normal Polarity	It's also known as negative polarity—SEGY. Increase in impedance in the trough (white (-) value).

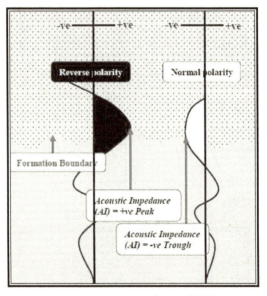

Figure VI-15: Reverse and normal polarity
(courtesy of Global Data Subsurface)

To recap, we said that the black/white curves (lobes) are a representation of the "slowness" and the "softness" of each of the Earth layers.

The "slow/hard" or "soft/hard" depends on two factors in all the layers, i.e., velocity and density, respectively.

We go a bit further with this. When we combine the two "ingredients" v (velocity), * ρ (density), we'll get what the geophysicists call AI (acoustic impedance).

Remember this:
AI = v * ρ

Refer to **Appendix F: The birth of a seismic trace.**

For seismic data from offshore surveys, it is easy to determine the polarity based on the seabed.

PHASE MODE

Phase is a representation of the seismic lobes at the formation boundaries.

For zero phase, the seismic amplitude peak/trough is on the crossing of two boundaries.

For the minimum phase, the seismic amplitude peak/trough is within the formation or putting in another way, the crossing at the formation boundaries are at the point of inflexion in the seismic trace.

| Minimum phase | The peak/trough denotes the center of a formation. |
| Zero phase | The peak/trough denotes the top/base of a formation. |

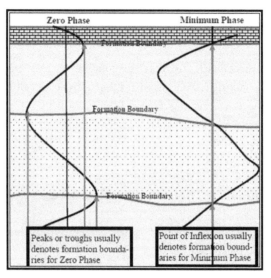

Figure VI-16: Minimum and zero phase
(courtesy of Global Data Subsurface)

SEISMIC ELEVATION DATUM

The datum of the elevation above time = 0ms due to weathered layer which followed the topology of the surface.

Please refer to **Figure III – 18.**

3D SEISMIC SURVEY

i	Line(INLINE)	vii	Sample rate
ii	Trace (CROSSLINE)	viii	Data format
iii	Bin size	ix	Polarity
iv	XY–Easting & Northing	x	Phase mode
v	Lat & Lon	xi	Elevation datum
vi	Record length		

LINE (INLINE) – IL

i	Range	ii	Incremental

TRACE (CROSSLINE) – XL

i	Range	ii	Incremental

BIN SIZE

i	6.25m × 6.25m	iii	25m × 25m
ii	12.5m × 12.5m	iv	Any combination of the above three

There is another thing to take note.

Normally in the Acquisition or Processing reports, we will be furnished of the survey details inclusive of the bin sizes plus the XY of the four corners.

If somehow upon defining the survey based on the report and the bin sizes do not look right as shown as an examples in the table below;

	Correct survey bin size		Wrong survey bin size	
	Inline	Xline	Inline	Xline
Example 1	6.25	12.5	6.04	12.15
Example 2	25	25	25.75	26.36

Check again the XY coordinates of the four corner points in the report. Still, a problem then used the XY in the trace header. This seldom happened if there is a report. Normally is the case when we restored from backups given by partners or from old project without any supportive documents

Example 1;

The wrong survey is defined smaller than the original surey.

For the Inline, the difference is 0.21m which means that for every 1000 inlines we have an offset of 21m, for every 2000 inlines the offset is 42m and for every 3000 inlines the offset is 63m from the first inline.

For the Xline, the difference is 0.35m which means that for every 1000 xlines, the offset is 35m, for every 2000 xlines the offset is 70m and for every 3000 xlines the offset is 105m from the first xline.

If a well is to be proposed than the offset from the right location will be in the range of ~41 to 125m for surveys having 1000 – 3000 inlines and xlines.

<u>Example 2</u>;

The wrong survey is defined bigger than the original survey.

For the Inline, the difference is 0.75m which means that for every 1000 inlines we have an offset of 75m, for every 2000 inlines the offset is 150m and for every 3000 inlines the offset is 225m from the first inline.

For the Xline, the difference is 1.36m which means that for every 1000 xlines, the offset is 136m, for every 2000 xlines the offset is 272m and for every 3000 xlines the offset is 408m from the first xline.

If a well is to be proposed than the offset from the right location will be in the range of ~155 to 466m for surveys having 1000 – 3000 inlines and xlines.

This the one of the reasons for misties for ovelapping 3D3D surveys. Also when proposing for well location, we are surely to drill in the wrong location.

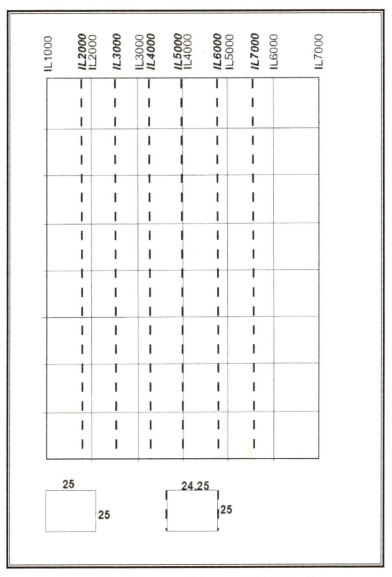

Figure VI-17: 3D survey with bin size 25 X 24.25 problem

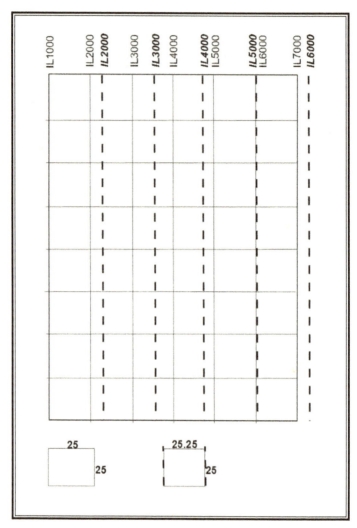

Figure VI-18: 3D survey with bin size 25 X 25.25 problem

XY

(1) These will define the survey(s) corner points.

(2) Even though the seismic traces coverage is polygonal, the survey is always defined in quadratic shape.

Please refer to page **93**.

LATITUDE AND LONGITUDE

Please refer to page **95**.

RECORD LENGTH

Please refer to page **95**.

SAMPLE RATE

Please refer to page **96**.

DATA FORMAT

Please refer to page **98**.

POLARITY

Please refer to page **100**.

PHASE MODE

Please refer to **101**.

SEISMIC ELEVATION DATUM

Please refer to page **102**.

FURTHER READINGS

1	Refer to Data Management Manuals from G&G software vendors.

VII – SEISMIC DATA LOADING

SET STANDARDS IN LOADING SEISMIC

POLARITY

Decide on a standard SEGY polarity convention:

* **Reverse polarity**
  (Peak = black (+ ve) and trough = white (- ve))

  or

* **Normal polarity**
  (Peak = white (- ve) and trough = black (+ ve))

PHASE

This is very subjective, as on land most SEGY output is near minimum phase, and in marine, the output is near *zero phase*. In reality, all seismic data are mixed phases.

Not to worry, choose one.

SAMPLE RATE

For time – seismic;

(1) VSP is 1ms.
(2) High-Resolution seismic is 2ms.
(3) Normal seismic is 4ms.

For depth – seismic;

(1) Normal seismic is 5m (~15ft) or 10m (~30ft)

Seldom you come across normal time - seismic having **3ms** as the sampling rate BUT it does exist.

RECORD LENGTH

Record length varies from surveys to surveys.

In time – seismic can be as deep as 15000m (~45000ft) and shallow as 4000m (~12000ft).

During loading, the record length can be reduced *but* be careful not to load exceeding the original record length registered.

For example, if the original record length registered is 7500ms, we can load 7500ms or less. But we cannot load more than 7500ms as there will be a wrap around on all the traces with the presiding traces. See Figure-7.1 of wrap around traces.

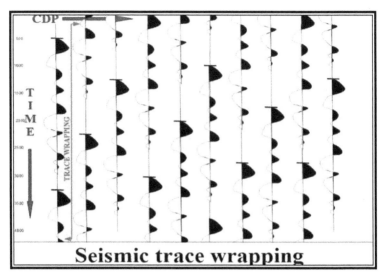

Figure VII-1: Pseudo traces wrapping around due to loaded record length exceeding original record length

SAMPLE FORMAT

Normally nowadays, 3D seismic are loaded with 32-bit format. But always check the histogram for the whole seismic dataset. The amplitude range ± will help to decide which format to be used in loading.

Scenarios:

(1) If the amplitude ranges are less than ± 128, load the seismic as 8-bit.
(2) If the amplitude ranges are less than ±32000, load the seismic as 16-bit.
(3) If the amplitude ranges are more than ± 32000, we have the options of loading the seismic in 16-bit or 32-bit.
(4) But for 2D seismic from old vintages either load as 8-bit or 16-bit but preferably 8-bit.

3D SEISMIC LOADING

• PROJECT CREATION

Within a project or projects, multiple surveys can coexist. All software provides utilities to create projects and subprojects.

• SURVEY DEFINITION

(1) INLINE (IL–Line) Range: IL (min)–IL (max).
(2) XLINE (XL–Trace) Range: XL (min)–XL (max).
(3) ILXL increment.
(4) XY of the 4 corner points of the survey as indicated in the SEGY trace header byte location 73 (for X coordinates) and 77 (for Y coordinates). This depends also on individual servicing contractor outputting the SEGY data.

---

*An example: If the survey has an increment = 2 in IL, XL or both, e.g., but loaded every 1, the traces or lines are displayed every other traces/lines. See **Figure VII.2**.*

*The survey has to be redefined again with the correct increment. See **Figure VII.3**.*

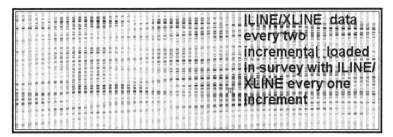

Figure VII-2: Iline/Xline has data with incremental = 2 loaded in survey defined with incremental = 1

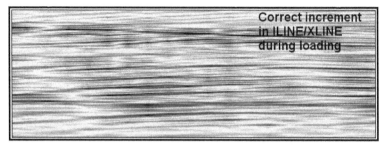

Figure VII-3: Iline/Xline loaded with correct incremental

2D SEISMIC LOADING

i	Line name	iii	Shot points – SP
ii	XY coordinates	iv	SP–seismic trace correspondence (or relationship)

Old vintage scenarios:

(1) No navigation in the SEGY trace header *but* SOL and EOL of lines are in the EBCDIC header each with the coordinates XY, load them. It will be represented as a straight line until a true navigation data are available.

(2) No SP but only trace in the TRACE header, use the trace as SP as well thus SP-TRACE relation is 1:1.

(3) No SP or TRACE (CDP) numbering in the SEGY headers especially the trace header, then you look in any of the bytes location where the numbering is increasing or decreasing linearly. Here, one can manipulate the numbering system using the multiplicity option in the SEGY utility option.

(4) If in the TRACE HEADER there is no definitive CDP/SP numbering, it is safe to use the same numbering sequence as the traces, unless there is a survey report or document to identify the SP range. In this case, we will have an equally spaced SP – TRACE numbering set.

(5) At times, we will find a situation whereby we have XY (source) and XY (group) in the byte locations. Choose the XY for the source.

SEISMIC PROJECT CREATION

3D

• FOUR (CORNER POINTS)

(1) Locate the information (at times) in the EBCDIC header.

(2) Or in the TRACE header byte locations 73 and 77 (X-Y coordinates).

(3) Bin size, i.e., the IL interval and the XL interval.

It is a good practice to draw (or sketch) the survey area defined by the four corner points highlighting, especially the inline. These will help in knowing the area defined and the orientation of the IL and also the XL.

E.g., let's get an example of a survey definition and a simple sketch.

Point (grid)	INLINE	XLINE	X	Y
1	49680	2419	180212.58	8550084.29
2	30400	2419	179802.89	8598233.37
3	49680	9583	269762.43	8550792.23
4	30400	9583	269352.74	8598991.31

Table VII-1: Survey #1 acreage definition

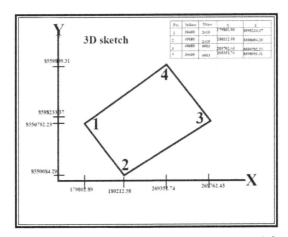

Figure VII-4: A sketch of a 3D survey based on the survey definition

113

For a bit of practice, refer to **Appendix G: Training to load 2D3D seismic data using OPENDTECT G&G software**.

Note that whether it is a 2D or 3D loading, please display the loaded dataset in both variable density and variable area.

If you are adventurous enough, display other attributes as well for example phase, frequency, similarity or coherency, plus others within the O&G software, just to be prepared for 'some' users.

Now in variable density, this will not show up except displayed in variable area, i.e., amplitude clipping. This will probably be seen in old dataset. Or it can also happen that after running the histogram, we decided to do away with all the high amplitudes.

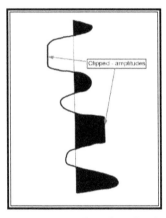

Figure VII-5: Clipped amplitude

Revision for Amplitude dynamic ranges;

(1) *-128<Amp<+128, load the seismic as 8-bit integer.*
(2) *--32000<Amp<-+32000, load the data as 16-bit integer.*
(3) *--430000000000<Amp<-+430000000000, load the data as 32-bit integer*

SEISMIC DISPLAY

	Mode	Seismic displays
1	Wiggle	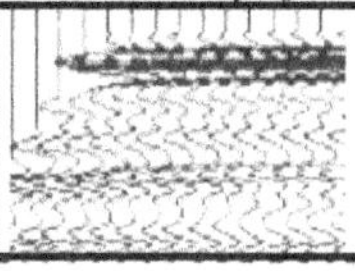
2	Wiggle/Positive fill	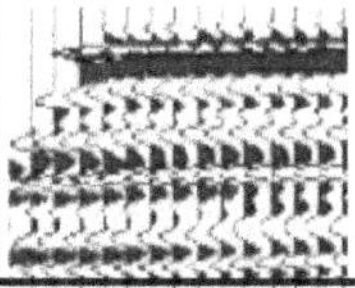
3	Wiggle/Negative fill	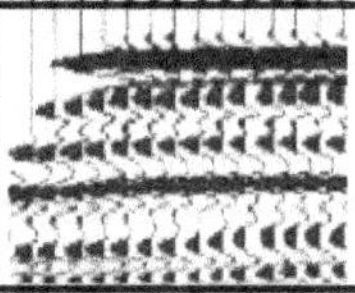
4	Variable density	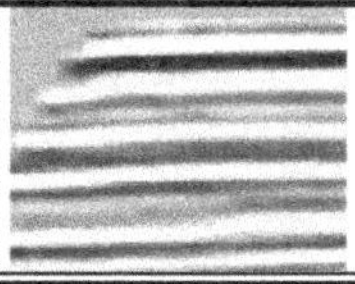

Figure VII-6: Seismic display modes

FURTHER READINGS

1	Refer to data management manuals from G&G software vendors.

VIII – DATA HARMONIZATION

We always like to use this catchy phrase *"data cleaning"* and at times *"data harmonization."*

OBJECTIVE

It's nothing more than a series of steps or processes to make our data repository clean.

Putting it in a professional way, data harmonization is sequential steps or processes whereby:

(1) The data are checked thoroughly.
(2) Corrected where necessary.
(3) And approved for final usage.

So in other words, a systematically performed task of validating the seismic data and if necessary, applied correction(s) with the assurance that upon delivery to the user(s) the data are ready to be worked upon.

As we are *only* dealing with *seismic data*, we'll stay focused *only* on the seismic.

Now is a good time to apply our "**Eight Golden Rules of Data Management**" in total or part of it.

DATA CHECKING

What to check in seismic data or surveys?

ARE THE SURVEYS (2D OR 3D) DEFINED CORRECTLY WITH THE RIGHT COORDINATE REFERENCE SYSTEMS (CRS)?

You might have "beautiful" seismic staring at your face but wrongly placed . . . what worse scenario can it be than this. . . drilling at the wrong location?

Refer to **IV. Coordinate Reference Systems**, **Exercises** on correct coordinates.

ARE THE OVERLAP 3D3D SEISMIC SURVEYS TYING TO ONE ANOTHER?

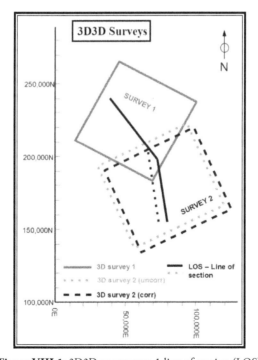

Figure VIII-1: 3D3D survey map-1 line-of-section (LOS)

Figure VIII-1 shows a map with two (2) 3D surveys overlapping each other. The dotted 3D survey – 2 is the original loaded prior to CRS correction. The line-of-section between the two 3D surveys is shown in black with the dotted line representing the LOS traversing the uncorrected survey.

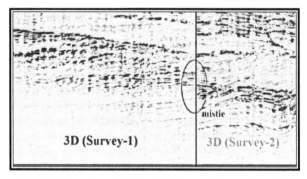

Figure VIII-2: Example – 3D3D mistie between Survey–1 and Survey–2

Figure VIII-2 shows a mistie between two 3D surveys overlapping each other. See feature within the circle.

This is obviously showing either:

(1) Both or one of the surveys are loaded with the wrong coordinates.
(2) Both or one of the surveys are defined in the wrong CRS.
(3) Also, but rarely, both have different sampling rates.

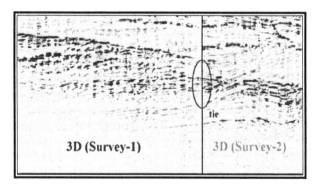

Figure VIII-3: Example – 3D3D tie after correction
between Survey-1 and Survey–2

Figure VIII-3 shows the tie between the two (2) 3D surveys after correction. This is based on the geological continuity between the two surveys.

ARE THE OVERLAPPED 2D3D SEISMIC SURVEYS TYING TO ONE ANOTHER?

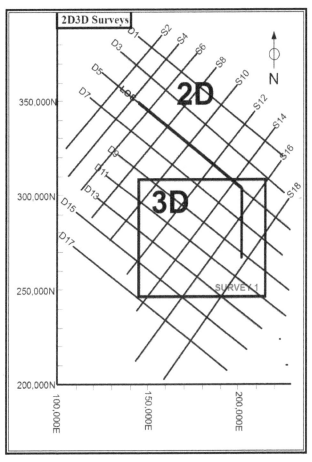

Figure VIII-4: 2D3D survey map

Figure VIII-4 shows a 2D3D survey map with a LOS traversing across both the 2D and 3D surveys.

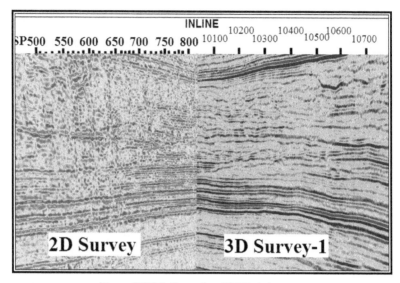

Figure VIII-5: Example – 2D3D tie between
2D line D5 and 3D Survey – 1

Figure 8-5 shows 2D3D ties which are more definitive by showing the continuity in the geology

This can only be the results of:

(1) Correct navigation loaded.
(2) Correct CRS applied.

Mind that if we zoom-in at the 2D3D intersection, a slight mistie is pronounced as the 2D seismic and the 3D seismic have different processing parameters to ensure exact tie.

ARE THE 2D2D SEISMIC LINES (VINTAGES, I.E., DIFFERENT YEARS OR DIFFERENT BLOCKS OR ACREAGE) TYING TO ONE ANOTHER?

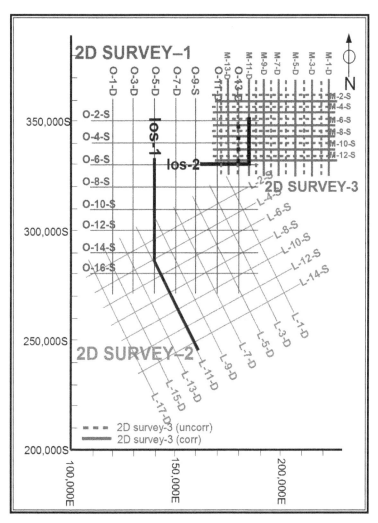

Figure VIII-6: 2D2D survey map—an example

Figure VIII-6 shows a map of three (3) 2D surveys, consisting of two (2) correct surveys and one (1) uncorrected survey—2D Survey-3 (due to wrongly loaded navigation or the CRS wrongly applied).

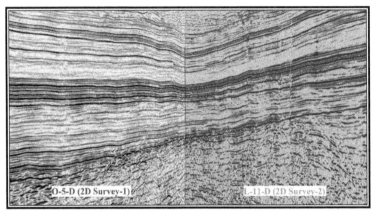

Figure VIII-7: 2D line O-5-D in traverse view
with line of intersection: L-11-D (los-1)

Figure VIII-7 shows intersection and tie point between two lines:
O-5-D (2D Survey-1) and L-11-D (2D Survey-2) depicted by line-of-
section (los-1).

These are also due to:

(1) Correct navigation loaded.
(2) Correct CRS applied.

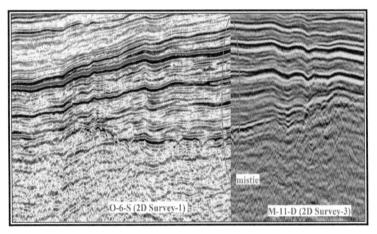

Figure VIII-8: 2D2D mistie before navigation
correction 2D Survey–1 and Survey–3 (los – 2)

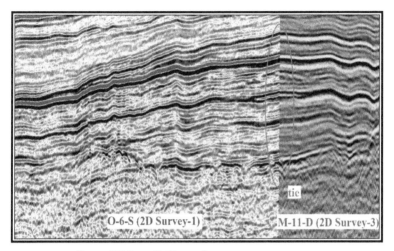

Figure VIII-9: 2D2D tie after navigation correction
between 2D Survey-1 and Survey – 3 (los – 2)

The examples above show two (2) 2D lines of different vintages intersecting each other before correction in **Figure VIII-8** and after correction in **Figure VIII-9**.

And the reasons are obvious before correction:

(1) The 2D line(s) loaded with wrong navigation.
(2) Or the datum for the survey(s) is defined wrongly.

DUPLICATED SURVEYS

This can happen to:

Users working each within a specific seismic time window or within specific area.

In the old days, software cannot handle specific requests like the above. Thus, multiple projects/surveys have to be generated to cater for each user.

Nowadays, you can work with one project or survey with different scenarios, i.e., each user working within specific area.

Thus, it is the prerogative of us, the data managers, to combine all the information into one single project/survey.

HAVING SURVEYS NOT ACTIVE FOR 'AGES' I.E. FOR QUITE SOMETIME?

You probably have come across loaded surveys that have not been touched for more than three to four years but are still residing on the systems or servers.

Before they became "fossilized" in your systems better go through these "mummified" surveys, clean them up, archive them, and delete them from your systems.

ARE THE FINAL SEISMIC VOLUMES CORRECTLY SCALED?

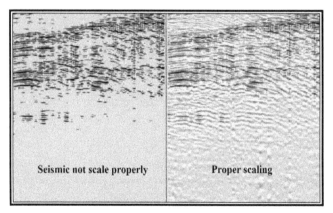

Figure VIII-10: (LHS) Seismic data do not scale with the correct bit before loading: (RHS) after rescaling with the correct bit

When rescaling, one should know from which scale bit to which scale bit. From the histogram applied to the loaded seismic, we will know the amplitude dynamic range to scale down our current volume.

The seismic in **Figure VIII-10** was loaded as 32-bit but in actual fact, it is 8-bit data based on the amplitude range.

Refer to **VI. SEGY Header Analysis**.

ARE THERE DUPLICATED SEISMIC VOLUMES (8-BIT DATASET, 16-BIT DATASET, 32-BIT DATASET)?

In the early workstations, seismic data are loaded in 8-bits. Then as workstations went through advancement or development, seismic data are loaded in 16-bits or 32-bits.

Thus, remnants of the 8-bits should be totally deleted, if and only if, we have 16-bit or 32-bit data of the same volume set.

Also, now with cheaper disks and space are of no issue, our friends, the users, i.e., the interpreters, are also loading seismic data (from where they obtained their SEGY, only them know, with their "skill" in data loading). They are working on 32-bits, but they want to see the 16-bit version.

Hunt for these volumes and delete them only after consultations with the users

ARE THERE ANY UNWANTED GENERIC SEISMIC VOLUMES GENERATED BY THE USERS THEMSELVES E.G., PHASE, FREQUENCY, SPECTRAL DECOMPOSITION, AND OTHER SEISMIC ATTRIBUTES THAT HAVE NOT BEEN DELETED?

Users in the midst of their work, in delineating channels, leads, etc. will generate tons of volumes in the form of frequency (instantaneous, response), phase (instantaneous, response), spectral frequencies, reflection strength, spectral decomposition, etc.

These are mostly on trial-and-error basis and will be not used at all after this. Normally, the right usable volumes will have the name changed to fit the project involved in order not to be deleted.

LAST BUT NOT LEAST, SEISMIC VOLUMES HAVE NAMES GENERATED *BUT* NO SEISMIC DATA APPEAR, I.E., 0 (ZERO) KB

This is also another common thing. During the loading of seismic volumes, something happened, and the loading stopped.

The seismic datasets were deleted due to space constraints but the pointer to the seismic header still exists.

It is always a good practice to delete these seismic data through the menu utilities rather than manually.

The project data harmonization is not a one-time thing. The process has to be performed regularly at intervals say every 5 years. But the amount of work done will not be as tedious and cumbersome as the first time started.

FURTHER READINGS

	Title	Author	Date	Website
1	Modern Marketing Essntial Guide: Data Management	Oracle		http://demand.eloqua.com/

IX – BACKUP –
ARCHIVE – RESTORE

Now that we have performed a good job in collecting data, arranging data and loading data with correct navigational parameters but if the backups are not carried out professionally, the organization/company loses everything—not only *data* but also time and money.

This is particularly important as nowadays, we're dealing with terabytes and petabytes of datasets, not megabytes or gigabytes.

We should be wary not only of the disks/storage capacity but also of the strategy in which data are stored. The planning of the storage strategy will have impact in the disaster recovery in the near future if any.

So in this chapter, we are going to discuss the followings:

(1) The objective of performing backup, restore, archive, and delete.
(2) The backup process in detail.
(3) The archive process in detail.
(4) The delete process in detail.
(5) The restore process in detail.

OBJECTIVES

(1) To ensure the safety of the data, an hourly, daily, weekly, monthly and yearly backup are performed.
(2) To backup and archive project(s) because the project(s) will not be revisited for years in the future until the proposed project re-evaluation or other special purposes.
(3) To revisit past projects for upgrading to new versions.

Ensure that the storage facilities (warehouse, godowns, storage center) for keeping these media are conducive for storage. This is to ensure the long lifespan of the media.

BACKUP

(1) Write a simple script to backup UNIX files or flat files. Then slowly extend the algorithm to be more "robust." This is for scriptwriting geeks.
(2) For more sophisticated backups, there are numerous backup software (project management or data management software) in the market.
(3) Likewise, there are software to restore and archive for Linux and Window-based systems.
(4) Ensure that there are log files to check what were backed-up.
(5) Ensure that each schedule for backup is checked, failing which an alert pop-up window will display the failures or by sending an e-mail to the system administrator.
(6) For any backup systems implemented, ensure that the restore can also be performed manually in case the automatic routine malfunctioned.

A question still remains though, how do we handle seismic data where the volumes can be up to 500 GB to 1 Tb, depending on the size of the survey(s)?

Currently, a number of G&G software have a way to compress the loaded data.

But these data are in internal storage format for that particular software. Output these into SEGY format, and the volume size multiplies!

Also with the increase in working volumes, seismic data have to be accessed across servers. And the speed of accessing these seismic data depends on the following factors:

(1) The way the data is sorted in the storage media (disks) on the server(s).
(2) The size of the disks where the data reside.
(3) The system design of the server(s) and the workstation(s) setup.
(4) The network design of the system setup.
(5) The database design on the servers(s).
(6) The power of the server(s) and the workstation(s).

ARCHIVE

(1) Projects finalized and closed are normally backed-up and deleted.
(2) But the data in the projects have to be "cleaned" first prior to backup. See **VIII: Data Harmonization**.
(3) Backup media are normally DLT, LTO, DVD, and CD.
(4) It is a good practice to revisit these archive datasets periodically to determine the data accessibility and also, as mentioned earlier, to upgrade the archived media to the latest version.
(5) The purpose of the media upgrading is;

   • to save space and
   • to align with current best technology.

DELETE

(1) Project(s) are deleted when they are finalized after total project archived is performed.

(2) But prior to that, approval on such action should come from the user(s) department or team.

(3) If using a commercial project or data management software, one is advised to use the deletion mode in the menu setup.

This will also ensure safe and complete deletion of the links to the project. If not, some hidden files which are related to the dataset or project will be left "dangling," and the processes of these will still be running in the background. These "zombie" processes will lead to error messages popping up and, at times, will eventually stop the software from executing properly.

(4) Make sure the deletion log file(s) are generated for future references.

(5) One can also record the deletion as a task in the daily record book and ensure its inclusion in the weekly or monthly report.

(6) If the deleted routine is script written in-house, ensure that all data with respect to the project(s) in question are deleted, and no loose ends are left behind.

RESTORE

(1) Performed when the data/projects are to be revisited.

(2) To test the accessibility of the data in the storage media.

(3) To upgrade the storage media to the latest technology available.

(4) As mentioned earlier, a "test restore" should be performed once a while (say twice a year) to ensure that what were programmed to backup are totally restored, i.e., fully functional.

EXTERNAL SERVICES

Nowadays, there are companies offering services to perform all of the above especially with the new technique in the industry known as "cloud backup."

But this new technique is yet to be proven for backing-up seismic data which are up to 500GB or more in size.

FURTHER READINGS

1	Most IT books on the open shelves pertaining to systems management have these topics—backups, restores, and archives.

APPENDICES

A: INDEX

B: GLOSSARY

The meaning of . . . in layman's term	
A	
acoustic impedance	The product of two attributes, i.e., density (ρ) and velocity (v) within a formation, AI=ρv.
AME	Advanced Metal Evaporated
	The tape offers expanded recording capacity and low abrasivity, reducing mechanical wear. (http://www.datatechstore.com)
amplitude	The energy strength of the wave/trace that reflected from a boundary between two formations depending on the density and velocity of each formation.
angle stack	Stacking (or combining) the amplitudes through various angle in seismic gather.
archiving	Project or data stored away in media prior to removing from the system.
ASCII	American Standard Code Information Interchange
	A form of meta or text file.
AVO	Amplitude versus Offset
	The amplitude is analyzed as the distance varies from the origin.

The meaning of . . . in layman's term

B	
basemap	A display of elements or items, e.g., 2D or 3D lines or bathymetry (depth of sea bottom), etc. from top view or birds' eye view in a scaled-form. Use interchangeably with map.
bits	The smallest entity or unit of data sample.
boreholes	The hole that started with the same location of any well *but* along the way deviates to pacify targets.
BPI	Bits-Per-Inch.
	A form of storage density on a particular media.
byte	A string of bits. 1 byte = 8 bit.

C	
CDP	Common Depth Point
	The halfway point where the wave from the source hit a near horizontally flat-plane (*not* dipping plane) and being reflected to the receiver.
CMP	Common Mid-Point
	The halfway point above the CDP for the sources and receivers
compressed data	Data stored or copied onto a medium with storage mode denser than the source thus more data can be saved.
convolution	The process whereby the seismic amplitude are only depending on velocity and density and denoting geological layering.
coordinate reference system	The coordinate system used on a planar surface which is localized with the XY axes known as the easting and northing.
CROSSLINE	The points where seismic data were acquired along the traverse (INLINE) whereby during processing generating another traverse line perpendicular to the INLINE. This can only be done in 3D.

The meaning of . . . in layman's term	
D	
data archive	A process to back-up every file in a project prior to project removal from the system.
data backup	A process done regularly or at uniform intervals to safe either all the files in a project or files that have been modified within the project currently alive on the system.
data collection (gathering)	A process to search/gather/collect information to start a project, e.g., seismic data for 2D or 3D or 4D.
data delete	A process to remove data from online system.
database development	Process of improving the database.
data input	A process to load data into system.
data manager	Professional data handle and manage data in a system.
data restore	A process to reload data back into the system.
data validation	A process to verify data integrity and wellness.
Deconvolution	Process of making the seismic amplitude more narrow thus making the boundaries of the geological layers more refined.
dipline	Seismic line orientation that is perpendicular to the subsurface fault plane(s).
E	
EBCDIC	Extended binary coded decimal interchange code
	A form of meta or text file

The meaning of . . . in layman's term	
F	
fast-track	Pre-final seismic data with minimal seismic processing sequence which can be mapped/interpreted.
faults	A line of weaknesses in the subsurface that will result in displacement either through compression or tension.
FD	Floppy disk.
field	Area already has oil/gas wells currently on production.
film	One of the media used for data storage in prior to using tapes media.
flow	A process in a project that has a start and an ending.
fold(s)	No. of times the same location or point is being covered/detected by the signals. In this case here, it's either the geophone or the hydrophone.
G	
geology	The study of the Earth using chemistry-based principles.
geophysics	The study of the Earth using physics-based principles.
gigabyte (GB)	Unit of computer storage ~1024×1000 KB
H	
horizon	A demarcation on the seismic traces depicting geological boundaries.
I	
IDRC	Improved data recording capability
IEC	International Electro-technical Commission
	It sets an international standards and conformity assessment for all electrical, electronic, and related technologies. (http://www.iec.ch).
INLINE	The set lines traverse during the process of acquiring seismic data.

The meaning of . . . in layman's term	
J	
JEDEC	Joint Electron Devices Engineering Council
	It sets a Global Standards for the Microelectronics Industry. [http://www.jedec.org].
K	
kilobyte (KB)	1024 bytes.
L	
LAS	Log ASCII Standard
	A form of meta or text format.
LAT	latitude
	Imaginary lines that encircle the Earth horizontally with the largest diameter at the Equator. Lines to the north of the Equator are denoted with °N and lines to the south of the Equator are denoted with °S, e.g., 45°N or 80°S.
lease-sale evaluation	To study in detail the area before committing to signing MOU (memorandum of understanding)
leads	Areas where there are signs of potential oil/gas but not tested.
LON	longitude
	Imaginary lines encircling the Earth vertically passing through both the north and south poles. Line passing through Greenwich in UK known as GMT is denoted with 0°. Lines to the east of the GMT are denoted with °E and to the west are denoted with °W, e.g., 15°W or 110°E.
M	
MB	megabyte
	Unit of storage ~1024 KB.

The meaning of . . . in layman's term	
P	
papers	One of the old media modes in displaying seismic data prior to the advent of workstation.
polarity – normal	Increase in impedance on a negative axis.
polarity – reverse	Increase in impedance on a positive axis.
post-stack	After stacking (or combining traces)
pre-stack	Before stacking (or combining traces)
projected coordinates	Coordinate projected from global system in LATLON to Cartesian coordinate in easting and northing.
prospect	An area tested to have commercial oil/gas reserves but not yet produced.
S	
SEGY	Society of Exploration Geophysicist
seismic	Wave energy passing through the Earth detected at the surface due to natural or un-natural source(s).
seismic acquisition	The operation where seismic data been acquired in the fields.
seismic correlations	Seismic tie from 2D lines to 3D INLINE/CROSSLINE or vice-versa and also from one 2D vintage to another vintage.
seismic data	Data acquired from the subsurface using sound energy to depict the geology of the Earth in terms of traces and amplitudes.
seismic data management	How seismic data are being handled from acquisition until archiving.
seismic datum	Reference datum where time (T) = 0 ms
seismic interpretation	The seismic data were mapped based on distinct reflectors which also depict the boundaries of different geological surfaces or formations.

The meaning of . . . in layman's term	
seismic processing	The steps/flows in manipulating seismic data from the raw seismic data taken from the field tapes (SEGD format) up to the final product, i.e., processed seismic (SEGY format) for users to analyze and interpret.
seismic survey	The mode by which seismic data have been acquired.
seismic traverse	To follow seismic from one 2D line to another and also from one 2D line to one 3D INLINE or CROSSLINE.
SI	International System of Units, e.g., meters, kilograms, etc.
spheroid	An equivalent shape of the Earth.
storage media	Physical space/medium to store data
strikeline	Seismic line orientation parallel to the subsurface fault plane(s).
survey 4D	An equivalent to 3D survey but with time-lapse.
survey 3D	A survey that display the subsurface seismic in 3-dimensions, i.e., XY (inline/crossline) and Z (timeslice).
survey 2D	A survey that displays the seismic along the line of traverse, i.e., the 2D lines. Seismic in between the 2D lines cannot be displayed.
T	
tapes	A type of storage media. See Chapter 2.
TB	terabytes
	1024×1000×1000 KB
U	
uncompressed data	Data stored or copied onto a medium with the same storage mode as the source.

The meaning of . . . in layman's term	
V	
VSP	Vertical Seismic Profiling
	An operation to obtain seismic reading within a well whereby detectors are hung vertically with the source on the surface, i.e., can be near the well or placed a distance from the well. The 2second method is normally known as *Offset VSP*. Also, another method is where the source is moving away from the well at defined interval in length and distance. This is known as *Runaway VSP*.
W	
well correlations	To trace/tie geological boundaries from one well to the other
wells	Drilled holes to explore for hydrocarbons
workstation	Computer to process all job execution in the workplace/ work area.
well log curves	Series of graphical display of curves taken by set tools depicting geological information throughout the well. The display scales are in two modes: (1) linear scale, and (2) algorithmic scale.

C: THE BIRTH OF A SEISMIC TRACE

In **I: Overview** on page 19, in **Figure 1-1**, we saw examples of seismic sections or lines then a blow-up of a portion of the section and also a view of a single "trace."

Now let's go a bit further, only a bit (not byte), on how these traces came to be like we see them today on our workstation after loading. Refer to **VII. Seismic Data Loading**.

We'll make things as simple as possible.

And we are not going to touch on seismic data processing which is very big topic itself. Please refer to many of the seismic data processing books available on the shelves.

But for us, data managers, we'll only touch the surface of the "birth" of seismic traces.

In science, for us to understand a concept, we create a simple model; then from there on, we will vary the parameters to make a more complex model.

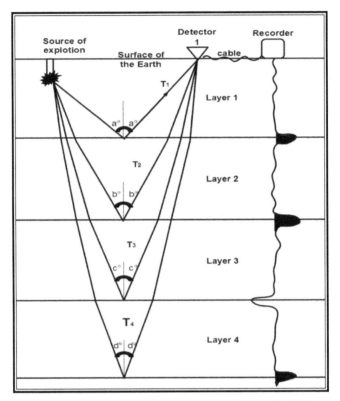

Figure F-1: Single source – single detector – single trace – Earth's layers

Figure F-1 shows a simple model of the Earth – we only depict four layers and, in this example, onshore, i.e., on land.

For offshore, the detectors, known as hydrophones, will be dangling on the sea/ocean surface.

Current technology—OBC (ocean bottom cable)—is whereby the hydrophones are laid on the bottom of the ocean.

We want to simplify things as much as possible so we can grasp the concept and whatsoever.

(1) There is a single source (dynamite, thumper, etc.) and a single detector (geophone) which will send the result to the recorder.

(2) When the source is detonated, it sends a series of waves or energy all around.

(3) Here, we picture the wave traveling in two dimensions only as shown in the **Figure F-1.**

(4) When these waves strike/hit/reach the boundary of layer 1 – 2, some waves are being reflected upward, while some waves still continue downward.

(5) Now, these waves have two parts: the incident part and the reflective part.

The incident part are the waves that are coming to hit the boundary while the reflective part are the waves that are up going which are about to hit the detector.

In this situation, we are particularly interested in the reflective wave since nearly all seismic acquisition performed in the oil and gas exploration industry are utilizing reflection seismic.

And the incident angle (a^0, b^0, c^0, d^0) must be equal to the reflection (a^0, b^0, c^0, d^0) . . . a bit of mathematics here . . . Phew!

(1) The wave that continues downward will also follow the same process as the above, i.e., upon reaching boundary layer **2 – 3,** boundary layer **3 – 4,** and boundary of bottom layer **4,** some waves will be reflected and hit the detector while some carry on going downward.

(2) And the detector will display notches (curves or lobes) to the left or right, an indicative of the arrival time from each boundary.

The example shows that the first notch will be **T0,** then followed by the notches of **T1**, **T2,** and **T3.** That is the reason why the time scale at the right side of a seismic section is also denoted as two-way time (TWT) in ms (millisecond).

Now we know that the notches are indicative of the boundaries between the Earth's layers. The left or the right notches (lobes) displays are what geophysicists call polarity. Cool!

As mentioned in Chapter 1: Overview, we'll get to know more about the wriggly nature of the traces in VI. **SEGY Header Analysis, Polarity.**

But now take a look at **Figure F-2** which shows a single source but three [3] detectors and resulting in three [3] traces.

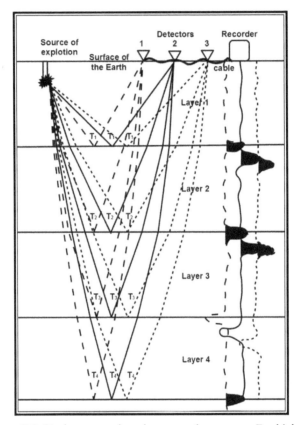

Figure F-2: Single source – three detectors – three traces – Earth's layers

To better understand the generations of the seismic traces, we put different line style to each of the three wave traces i.e.

continuous	————
dashed	—— —
fine dashed.	▪▪▪▪▪▪

The processes are the same as Figure F-1 but now we are dealing not with one trace but three traces:

(1) Releasing of the source
(2) The waves traveled and hit all the boundaries in the Earth model.
(3) Some waves are reflected while some are transmitted through (this wave is known refracted wave . . . do not get confused with reflected wave). See **Figure 2-5** and **Figure 2-6**.
(4) Detected by our three detectors, and
(5) Then comes out the three "beautiful" traces.

Notice anything about the three traces?

Yes, they are not aligned with each other. The trace lobes of the detector nearest to the source is shallower than the trace lobes of detectors two and three which are further away from the source.

They are reflected from the same boundaries, i.e., $1 - 2, 2 - 3, 3 - 4$, and 4.

But the travel time of the fine dashed wave is longer than that of continuous wave and that of continuous wave is longer than that of the dashed wave. Are we cool here?

But how do we get these lobes to be aligned with each other since all of them are reflecting from the same geological boundary?

Simply this is performed in the processing center and the process is known as normal move out (NMO).

But do refer to any seismic processing books if one is interested to join the seismic processing discipline.

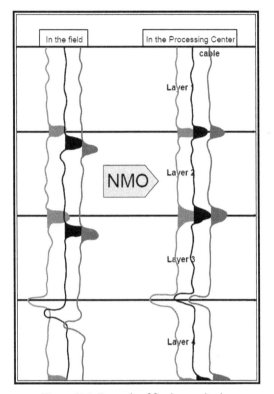

Figure F-3: Example of final trace display

In the real situation, we have the Earth with innumerous layers ranging from simple to complex scenarios, single or multiple source, multiples detectors (geophone or hydrophones), plus the environments range from kind to unforgiving. See **Figures III-4** and **III-5**.

And in the processing center, data processors will be fighting their own battle just to provide with the final processed seismic in SEGY format to be loaded and managed by Data Managers.

Also, here we simplified one trace to one SP.

In fact, one SP can have many traces called "gathers." From these gathers that in processing will "lump" into a single trace after going through "few" processes in the processing center.

Heed this:

- Samples ➜ Single Trace
- Traces ➜ Single Line (2D)
- Lines/Traces ➜ Seismic Volume (3D)

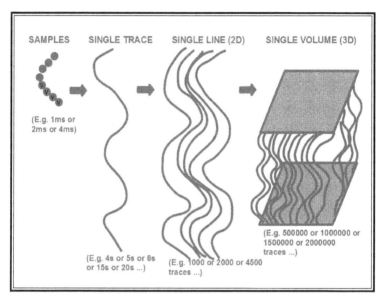

Figure F-4: Analogy from samples to seismic volume

This as simple as we can go. As scientists used to say "start from a simple model then develop into a more complicated one."

Ideally, we want our source and detector to be at the same point; thus, we'll then have the earth information directly beneath. It's impossible! And that's why we have the geometry of the source and the detectors.

The point where the signal reflects is known (get ready for another terrific term) as common depth point (CDP).

As the acquisition progresses, more signals will be reflected from the same CDP but from different geometry. Bear in mind that CDP only occurs at the horizontal flat plane.

In fact here, we depict one (1) SP one [1] trace. In actual life, under one [1] SP, we can have numerous traces.

This depends on "how many times" signals are detected by the same detector at the particular SP known as fold. The number of folds is dependent on the particular seismic survey designed.

Now, also another term that will be common to your ears is "gather." This is from the data gathering that the seismic processor will perform in velocity analysis. Enough or we'll get crazy!

These terms, fold and gather, are interchangeably used, so we shouldn't get confused as Confucius has left us a long time ago.

Refer to the following sites for further enhancement of our knowledge:

(1) www.xsgeo.com/course/acq.htm
(2) www.subsurfwiki.org/wiki/Gather
(3) …

D: KNOWN PROJECTION SYSTEMS

ALBERT EQUAL – AREA CONIC
AZIMUTHAL EQUIDISTANT
BORNE
CASSINI
CYLINDRICAL EQUAL-AREA
ECKERT IV
ECKERT VI
EQUIDISTANT CONIC
EQUIDISTANT CYLINDRICAL
IMW MODIFIED POLYCONIC
LAMBERT AZIMUTHAL EQUAL – AREA
LAMBERT CONFORMAL CONIC
LAMBERT TANGENTIAL
MERCATOR
MILLER CYLINDRICAL
NEW ZEALAND NATIONAL GRID
OBLIQUE MERCATOR
ORTHOGRAPHIC
POLAR STEREOGRAPHIC
POLYCONIC – AMERICAN
TRAVERSE MERCATOR
US STATE PLANE COORDINATE SYSTEM . . .
UNIVERSAL TRAVERSE MERCATOR
VAN DER GRINTEN

Table D-1: Examples of globally used projection systems

E: TO CONVERT DECIMAL DEGREES [DD] TO DEGREE, MINUTE, SECOND [DMS] VICE VERSA

DD (decimal degrees) conversion to DMS (deg, min, sec)

Example-1 is to convert LON **109.8765°E and** LAT **10.3456°N** to °
(DEG) ' (MIN) " (SEC)°.

(1) Let us first take longitude **109.8765°**E.
(2) **109** is the **degree**. Now we only got to convert **0.8765** to **minute** and **second**.
(3) **0.8765** multiply by **60** to convert to **minute**.
(4) Thus **0.8765 * 60 = 52.59** minute.
(5) **52** is minute and now remaining only the decimal part **0.59** minute to convert to second.
(6) **0.59** minute = **0.59 * 60 = 35.4** second.

So **109.8765 °E = 109° 52' 35.4"E**. QED.

Likewise, latitude **10.3456°N**

(1) **10** is the degree. Now only the remaining **0.3456°** to be converted to minute and second.
(2) First **0.3456** multiply by 60 to convert to minute.
(3) **0.3456 * 60 = 20.736"**.

(4) Thus **20** is the minute part. Now, what remains is only the **0.736** 'to be converted to second.

(5) **0.736 * 60 = 44.16**'

So **10.3456 °N = 10 ° 20' 44.16"N.** QED

DMS (degree, minute, second) conversion to DD (decimal degrees)

Now let us do the reverse conversion of Example 1.

Example-2 is to convert **109° 52' 35.4"E & 10 ° 20' 44.16"N** to LON LAT **DD°E**

(1) We maintain the value **109** which is already the deg.

(2) We have now **52' 35.4"**. We'll convert both to deg.

(3) **52** 'to convert to deg., **52** minutes are divided by **60** to give value in deg. as there are **60** minutes to a deg.

(4) **52/60 = 0.8667** (to 4 decimal places).

(5) Now to convert **35.4**"to deg., **35.4** seconds are divided by **3600** to give the value in deg. as there are 3600 seconds to a deg.

(6) **35.4/3600 = 0.0098** (to 4 decimal places).

(7) Now add up all the results.

(8) **109 + 0.8667 + 0.0098 = 109.8765**

So the final result = **109.8765°E** LON

Now you try to convert;

10 ° 20' 44.16"N to LAT **DD°N.**

Result =

F: SEISMIC TYPE

1	FAR ANGLE STACK
2	FASTTRACK
3	FULL_ANGLE_STACK
4	MIDDLE ANGLE STACK
5	MIGRATION FAR AMPLITUDE VERSUS OFFSET
6	MIGRATION FULL OFFSET
7	MIGRATION MIDDLE AMPLITUDE VERSUS OFFSET
8	MIGRATION NEAR AMPLITUDE VERSUS OFFSET
9	NEAR ANGLE STACK
10	POST STACK DEPTH MIGRATION
11	POST STACK TIME MIGRATION
12	PRE STACK DEPTH MIGRATION
13	PRE STACK TIME MIGRATION
14	RELATIVE ACOUSTIC IMPEDANCE

Table J-1: Standard nomenclatures of seismic volumes from processing centers

You'll receive data with numerous nomenclatures from partners (**Table J-2**), *but* mind you, they are part of the list in **Table J-1**.

1	DMOSTACK_KIRCHHOFF
2	FAR ANGLE
3	FULL FOLD STACK
4	FULL STACK TIME MIGRATION
5	GRADIENT VOLUME
6	INVERSION RESULTS - VPVS
7	INVERSION RESULTS - IP
8	LITHO PROBABILITY VOLUME – GAS SANDS
9	LITHO PROBABILITY VOLUME – WATER SANDS
10	LITHO PROBABILITY VOLUME – OIL SANDS
11	MID ANGLE STACK
12	NEAR ANGLE STACK
13	RELATIVE P IMPEDANCE

Table J-2: Client-specific nomenclatures of seismic volumes

Volumes 8 – 10 are special seismic processing outputs done using special processing techniques. These are performed on special request from users.

It is a good idea to start churning out standard nomenclature so one can keep track of the seismic datasets.

G: APPLIED SOFTWARE IN GENERATING THIS BOOK

Software	Developer	Website
Adobe Acrobat XI Pro 11.0.12	Adobe Systems Inc	www.adobe.com
GIMP (GNU Image Manipulation Program) 2.8.14	Spencer Kimball, Peter Matthis & the GIMP Development Team	www.gimp.org
MS Office	Microsoft Corp	www.microsoft.com
Open Office	Apache Software Foundation	www.openoffice.otg
OpendTect 5.0.8.	dGB Beheer BV	www.opendtect.org
Windows10	Microsoft Corp	www.microsoft.com
SegY Detective1.0	DECO Software Geophysical Co	www.radexpro.com
SeisSee2.22.5	Sergey Pavlukin, Dalmorneftegeofizika Geophysical Company (DMNG),	www.dmng.ru/seisview

Table G-1: Software used in producing the book

Also, try to get involved in these sites:

i	Toolbox	iii	nixCraft Linux/Unix
ii	SlideShare	iv	GeoScienceWorld

H: BUSINESS MODEL OF THE 8 – GOLDEN RULES OF SUBSURFACE DATA MANAGEMENT – TETRAMODEL11

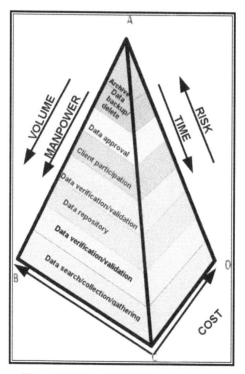

Figure H-1. Tetra-MODEL business model for subsurface data management

---

11 Business model by Global Data Subsurface

Figure H-1 displays a tetraMODEL in implementing the 8-golden rules of data management.

Each block or layer can be a project itself. As we can see the variables involved are dependant on each other i.e. volume, manpower, time and risk. And the base of each layer constitues the implemention cost.

For block or layer #1, we need more manpower because of bigger volumes of data plus more time as shown by the arrows but the risk are increasing as we go up the blocks or layers.

Meaning to say that we have undertaken various precautions or measures to pass the dataset from one block or layer to another upward. Thus the risk is also increasing as one escalates up the tetrahedron.

www.ingramcontent.com/pod-product-compliance
Lightning Source LLC
Chambersburg PA
CBHW051239050326
40689CB00007B/996